Collins
Webster's

175 YEARS OF DICTIONARY PUBLISHING

easy learning
ENGLISH
CONVERSATION

BOOK 1

HarperCollins Publishers
Westerhill Road
Bishopbriggs
Glasgow
G64 2QT

First edition 2012

Reprint 10 9 8 7 6 5 4 3 2 1 0

ISBN 978-0-00-745458-7

Collins ® is a registered trademark of
HarperCollins Publishers Limited

www.collinslanguage.com

A catalog record for this book is
available from the British Library

Typeset by Q2AMedia

Audio material recorded and produced
by Knowledgeworks

Printed in Great Britain by Clays Ltd,
St Ives plc

Editorial staff

Written by:
Elizabeth Walter and Kate Woodford

U.S. adaptation: Ellen Northcutt

Editor: Lisa Sutherland

For the publisher:
Lucy Cooper
Kerry Ferguson
Elaine Higgleton

contents

contents

Collins Easy Learning English Conversation: Book 1 is a completely new type of book for learners of English of all ages. It will help you to be able to speak in natural English like a native speaker, even if you have not been learning English for long.

To sound natural in English, you need to know both the words and the grammar of American English. However, it can be difficult to put these two things together and be sure that what you are saying sounds like natural English. *Collins Easy Learning English Conversation* has been carefully designed to give you whole sentences which you can use with confidence in all your conversations.

Collins Easy Learning English Conversation is made up of 14 units, each giving the language used in a particular situation, for instance shopping, traveling or talking about your health.

In each unit, the language is arranged by language task, for instance "saying what you want" or "making suggestions." Clear headings help you to find what you need. "Good to know" boxes give advice about things it is important to know.

There are lots of examples of the phrases, and the words in them are explained at the bottom of each page.

At the end of each unit is a page called "Listen for," which gives more useful phrases that you may hear or need to use in each situation. This is followed by a conversation, showing the phrases you have learned in a natural situation. You can listen to these conversations on the CD that comes with this book. The CD also contains some useful phrases you can listen to and then practise saying.

After the 14 units there is a chapter which arranges the phrases by language task. So, for example, all the phrases for "complaining" come together.

After this is a grammar section, giving useful advice on important grammar points, such as how to form tenses, and the differences between count and noncount nouns. Finally, there is a short section on useful phrasal verbs.

We hope *Collins Easy Learning English Conversation* will help you speak with confidence and success. For more information about Collins, please visit us at www.collinslanguage.com.

Talking to people

talking to people

Hello

You will often want to be able to talk to people and get to know them better. The phrases in this unit will help you talk to friends, family, people at work, and people that you meet.

Greetings

Use **Hello** as a general greeting. It is polite to say **Hello** to anyone in any situation.

> **Hello**, Jorge.
> **Hello**, Dr. Ahmed.

Use **Hi** in informal situations, for example when you are meeting friends.

> **Hi**, how are things with you?
> Oh **hi**, Adam. I didn't know you were coming.

Use **Good morning, Good afternoon**, or **Good evening** in slightly more formal situations, for instance if you meet a neighbor, or when you see people at work.

> **Good morning**, everyone. Today we are going to look at how to form questions.
> **Good afternoon**, Mr Kowalski.

> **GOOD TO KNOW!**
> In American English, there is no greeting starting with **Good** that is for the whole day.

Use **Goodbye** when you leave someone.

> **Goodbye**, Kara. Have a safe trip.

Goodbye is often shortened to **Bye**.

> **Bye**, everyone!

Use **Goodnight** when you are going to bed, or if someone else is going to bed.

> **Goodnight**, everyone. See you in the morning.

See you is an informal way of saying goodbye to someone you know you will see again.

> OK, I need to go now. **See you!**
> **See you** tomorrow!
> **See you** on Monday!

Introducing people

If you want to introduce someone to someone else, use **This is ...** . To introduce a group of people, use **These are ...** .

> **This is** my husband, Richard.
> **This is** Medina, my friend from school.

> **These are** my children, Andrew, Gordon, and Emma.
> **These are** my parents.

> **GOOD TO KNOW!**
> When you are introduced to someone, you can just say **Hello**,
> or in a slightly more formal situation, say **Pleased to meet you** or **Nice to meet you**.

Useful words

introduce   to tell people each other's names so that they can get to know each other

Talking about yourself

When you are talking to people, you will probably want to tell them some things about you. To say what your name is, use **I'm ...** or, in a slightly more formal situation, **My name's ...** .

> Hi, **I'm** Tariq. I'm a friend of Susie's.
> **I'm** Paul. I'm your teacher.
>
> **My name's** Johann.
> **My name's** Yuko. I'm Kazuo's sister.

If you want to say how old you are, use **I'm ...** . You can just say a number, or you can add **years old** after the number.

> **I'm** twenty-two.
> **I'm** thirty-seven **years old**.

> **GOOD TO KNOW!**
> We do not usually ask adults their age. If you want to ask a child his age, use **How old are you?**

To give general information about yourself, use **I'm ...** .

> **I'm** a friend of Paolo's.
> **I'm** married.
> **I'm** interested in old cars.

To talk about your work, use **I'm ...** with the name of a job, or **I work ...** to say something more general about what you do.

> **I'm** a doctor.
> **I'm** a bus driver.

Useful words

an adult	a fully grown person
married	having a husband or wife

I **work** for an oil company.
I **work** in Guadalajara.
I **work** as a translator.

> **GOOD TO KNOW!**
> If you want to ask someone what their job is, use **What do you do?**

To talk about where you live, use **I live** or **I'm from**. **I'm from** is also used to talk about where you were born and lived as a child, even if you do not live there now.

I **live** in Wales.
We live near Moscow.

I'm from Chicago, but I live in Phoenix now.
We're from Atlanta.

> **GOOD TO KNOW!**
> To ask someone where they live, use **Where do you live?** or
> **Where are you from?**

Asking for information

After saying **Hello** to someone, we usually ask about their health, by asking
How are you?

Hello, Jan. **How are you?**
It's great to see you, Anna. **How are you?**

> **GOOD TO KNOW!**
> To answer the question **How are you?**, use **I'm fine, thanks** or **I'm good, thanks.**
> If you aren't feeling well, you could say **Not great, really** or
> **Not too good, actually.**

Useful words
a translator   someone whose job is to change words into a different language

To ask someone you know about their life in general, use **How are things?** or **How are things with you?**

> Hello, Jan. **How are things?**
> Nice to see you, Karl. **How are things with you?**

When you are talking to someone, you may want to ask them about their life. Use **Tell me ...** for general questions.

> **Tell me** about your family.
> **Tell me** a little about yourself.
> **Tell me** about your job.

To ask someone to describe something, use **What's ... like?**

> **What's** your class **like?**
> **What's** your hometown **like?**
> **What's** your hotel **like?**

You can also use other general question words such as **Where ... ?**, **When ... ?** or **Why ... ?**

> **Where** is your office?
> **Where** do you work?
> **Where** are you staying?

> **When** did you meet Olga?
> **When** is his party?
> **When** do classes start?

> **Why** did you decide to become a teacher?
> **Why** did you go to Tokyo?
> **Why** did she stop painting?

Saying what you want to do

When you're talking to friends or people at work, you will often need to be able to talk about what you would like to do. Use **I'd like to ...** or **I want to ...** .

> **I'd like to** talk to him about his trip to Canada.
> **I'd like to** meet your family.
> **We'd like to** take you out for dinner.

> **I want to** leave by 5:00 this afternoon.
> **I want to** speak to her as soon as possible.
> **I want to** invite you all for dinner.

Making suggestions

One easy way of making suggestions to your friends and people at work is to use **We could ...** .

> **We could** ask Paul to join us.
> **We could** meet another time.
> **We could** meet at the Café de la Poste.

If you are eager to do something with your friends or people you work with, use **Let's ...** .

> **Let's** stay a little longer.
> **Let's** invite lots of people.
> **Let's** go to a restaurant later.

Useful words
invite   to ask someone to come to an event

If you want to make a suggestion and see if other people agree with you, use **Should we?**

> **Should we** see what George wants to do?
> **Should we** order a pizza?
> **Should we** ask Suri if she wants to come with us?

If you have a suggestion about something you could do, use **How about ... ?**

> **How about** going swimming?
> **How about** asking for some time off from work?
> **How about** sending him a text?

> **GOOD TO KNOW!**
> **How about + -ing**
> The verb that comes after **How about** must be in the -ing form.

Expressing opinions

When talking to people in a social or work situation, you may want to express your opinion of something. Use **I think ...** .

> **I think** Sonia's right.
> I really **think** it's too late to go to the movies.
> **I think** it's a great idea.

If you do not think something is true, use **I don't think ...** .

> **I don't think** Marc's coming.
> **I don't think** we should stay much longer.
> **I don't think** the restaurant is open on Mondays.

If you want to ask people if they think something is good or bad, use **What do you think of ... ?**

> **What do you think of** his latest movie?
> **What do you think of** this idea?
> **What do you think of** Mira's new apartment?

To ask someone if they think something is a good idea, use **What do you think about ... ?**

> **What do you think about** going out for dinner tonight?
> **What do you think about** inviting Eva?
> **What do you think about** having a party next weekend?

To agree with someone's opinion, use **I agree** or **You're right.** If you want to say who you agree with, use **with**.

> "This is a great restaurant." "**I agree**. We come here a lot."
> **I agree with** Nick.
> I completely **agree with** you!

> "We'll be late if we don't hurry." "**You're right**! Let's go!"
> I think **you're right**.
> Matt**'s right**.

If you do not agree with someone, you can use **I don't think so.**

> "The food here's delicious, isn't it?" "**I don't think so**. My soup isn't
>   very good."
> "Pierre's really nice, isn't he?" "**I don't think so**. He never speaks to me."
> "Traveling by train is really relaxing." "**I don't think so**. I prefer to fly."

Useful words
relaxing   making you feel more calm and less worried

Talking about your plans

To tell your friends and people at work about your plans, use **I'm going to ...** .

> **I'm going to** text Brenda.
> **I'm going to** tell him tomorrow.
> **I'm going to** have lunch with Ted.
> **We're going to** meet on Wednesday.

To ask someone about their plans, use **Are you going to ... ?**

> **Are you going to** go to the concert?
> **Are you going to** look for a new job?
> **Are you going to** take a taxi home?

Making arrangements

To make arrangements with a friend or someone you work with, use
We can ... .

> **We can** have lunch downtown.
> **We can** meet after work.
> **We can** go together.

To explain an arrangement, use **I'll ...** .

> **I'll** meet you outside the theater.
> **I'll** pick you up at seven o'clock.
> **I'll** text you when I'm ready.

Useful words

downtown	in or toward the center of a city
text message	a message that you write down and send using a cellphone
pick someone up	to collect someone from a place

To check if someone is happy with the arrangements, use **Is ... OK?**

> **Is** eight o'clock **OK?**
> **Is** it **OK** if I bring a pizza?
> **Is** it **OK** to bring Charlie?

Saying what you have to do

To tell your friends or people at work what you have to do, use **I have to ...** .

> **I have to** make a phone call.
> **I have to** stay home tonight.
> **We have to** be there at eight o' clock.

To ask what someone has to do, use **Do you have to ... ?**

> **Do you have to** give them an answer today?
> **Do you have to** go now?
> **Do we have to** bring something?

When you want to say that you should do something, use **I should ...** .

> **I should** call Anne.
> **You should** come and visit us.
> **I should** give you my cellphone number.

Useful words
a cellphone   a phone that you carry around with you

● **Listen for**

Here are some useful phrases which you may hear or use when you are speaking to friends or people at work.

Have you ever been to Athens?
How long are you staying in Seattle?
Your English is very good.
Are you married?
Do you have any children?
Do you come here often?
Are you enjoying it here?
Have you worked here for a long time?

Do you speak French?
Could you speak more slowly, please?
I'm sorry. I don't understand.
Could you repeat that, please?
Thank you for a lovely evening.
It was great to meet you.
I hope we'll see you again sometime.

Listen to the conversation: Track 1

Katie is at her friend Andrew's party. Scott introduces himself.

A Hi, I'm Scott. I'm a friend of Andrew's.

B Nice to meet you. Andrew's told me a lot about you.

A You work with him, don't you? What do you do, exactly?

B I'm a math teacher. What about you?

A I work for an IT company.

B Oh.... Where are you from?

A I'm from Brisbane, Australia.

B So what do you think of the weather here in Massachusetts? Is it too cold for you?

A Well, sometimes Brisbane can be *too* hot, but a little more sun here would be nice!

B Do you plan to visit more of New England?

A I'd like to travel all around the United States. There's so much to see — it's not easy to decide where to go.

B You're right. There are a lot of wonderful places to visit!

 Listen to more phrases and practice saying them: Track 2

Traveling

Have a good trip!

If you are traveling, these phrases will help you to find out how to get to places and do things, such as buy tickets. They will also help you to talk about traveling, in clear, natural English.

Talking about your plans

When you are traveling, you may want to tell people what you will do. For travel plans that you are sure of, use **I'm going to ...** . Use **Are you going to ... ?** to ask someone about their travel plans.

> **I'm going to** spend a day in Chicago.
> **I'm going to** take the train.
> Then **we're going to** go to Toronto.

> **Are you going to** travel together?
> **Are you going to** fly there?

To talk about your plans, you can also use **I plan to ...** .

> **I plan to** spend a few days in Boston.
> **I plan to** visit some friends.
> **She plans to** work while she's in Australia.

Use **Will you ... ?** to ask if someone is going to do something.

> **Will you** call us when you get there?
> **Will you** take much luggage with you?

Useful words

spend	to use your time doing something
take	to use a vehicle to go from one place to another
fly	to travel somewhere in an aircraft
visit	to go to see someone in order to spend time with them
work	to have a job and earn money for it
luggage	the bags that you take with you when you travel

To talk about something that you would like to do but are not sure that you will do, you can use **I hope to ...** .

> **I hope to** go to Bulgaria this year.
> **I hope to** spend some time in the mountains.
> **We hope to** take a tour of the islands.

To talk about a travel plan that is only possible, use **I might ...** .

> **I might** book a hotel for the night.
> **I might** come home earlier than planned.
> **I might** spend an extra week in Calgary.

Saying what you have to do

If it is important for you to do something while you are traveling, use **I have to ...** or **I need to ...** .

> **I have to** buy a ticket.
> **I have to** take the train to Berlin first.

> **I need to** get to the airport by ten o'clock.
> **We need to** call a taxi.

Useful words	
a mountain	a very high area of land with steep sides
a tour	a trip to an interesting place or around several interesting places
an island	a piece of land that is completely surrounded by water
book	to arrange to have or use something, such as a hotel room, at a later time
a hotel	a building where people pay to stay and eat meals
an airport	a place where airplanes come and go, with buildings and services for passengers
a taxi	a car with a driver who you pay to take you somewhere

Another way of saying that it is important that you do something is **I must ...** .
This is used only when it is necessary that you do something.

> **I must** be back by June 5th.
> **I must** take my passport.
> **You must** take your cellphone.

Saying what you want to do

To say what you want to do when you are traveling, use **I'd like to ...** .

> **I'd like to** rent a bike.
> **I'd like to** take the train.
> **I'd like to** change my ticket.

If you know that you do not want to do something, use **I don't want to ...** .

> **I don't want to** travel alone at night.
> **I don't want to** fly, if possible.
> **We don't want to** spend a lot on accommodations.

Making suggestions

If two or more people are trying to decide what to do when traveling,
use **We could ...** or **Let's**.

> **We could** take a taxi instead.
> **We could** ask Ryan to take us there.
> **Let's** leave tomorrow morning.

Useful words	
a passport	an official document that you have to show when you enter or leave a country
a cellphone	a telephone that you can carry around with you
rent	to pay the owner of something in order to be able to use it yourself
spend	to pay money for things that you want or need
accommodations	buildings or rooms where people live or stay

To suggest what someone else can do when they are traveling, use **You could ...** .

> **You could** rent an apartment in the city.
> **You could** take a boat there.
> **You could** buy a ticket online.

You can use **How about ... ?** to suggest what someone might do.

> **How about** taking an earlier flight?
> **How about** meeting them at the airport?
> **How about** taking a boat trip?

GOOD TO KNOW!

How about + -ing

The verb that comes after **How about** must be in the -ing form.

You can also use **Why not ... ?** to suggest what someone might do.

> **Why not** ask Milos to take you?
> **Why not** get up and go early tomorrow morning?
> **Why not** drive there?

Useful words

overnight	happening through the whole night or at some point during the night
an apartment	a set of rooms for living in, usually on one floor and part of a larger building
online	using the Internet
a flight	a trip in an aircraft
a trip	a journey that you make to a particular place and back again
get up	to get out of bed
drive	to control the movement and direction of a car or other vehicle

Asking for information

You may need to go to a particular place or building when you are traveling. Use **Is there ... ?** to ask if there is such a thing where you are. You may need to get someone's attention before you can ask them a question. Use **Excuse me** to do this.

> **Excuse me**, **is there** a garage near here?
> **Is there** a campsite near here?
> **Is there** anyplace that rents rooms?
> **Is there** a grocery store on this street?
> **Are there** any restaurants around here?

You may want to find out the way to do something, for example how to buy a ticket. Use **How do ... ?**

> Excuse me, **how do** I buy a ticket from this machine?
> **How do** I use this phone?
> **How do** I call a number in Mexico?
> **How do** we get to the station?

If you are looking for a place and you want information about how to find it, use **Where ... ?**

> **Where** is the train station?
> Excuse me, **where** is the ticket counter?
> **Where** can I buy a ticket?
> **Where** is the post office?

Useful words

a garage	a place where you can have your car repaired
a campsite	a place where you can stay in a tent
a room	a separate area inside a building that has its own walls
a machine	a piece of equipment that uses electricity or an engine to do a particular job
a ticket counter	the place in a station that sells tickets

You may need advice when there are many choices and you need to know the right one for you. Ask **Which ... ?**

> **Which** train do I take?
> **Which** bus goes downtown?
> **Which** platform does the train for Philadelphia leave from?
> Excuse me, **which** train goes to Barcelona?

If you want to ask a general question you can use **Is it ... ?**

> **Is it** this way?
> **Is it** near here?
> **Is it** far?
> **Is it** on the right?

If you want to know the time that something happens, ask **What time ... ?**

> **What time** does the train leave?
> **What time** do we get to Rio?
> **What time** do we arrive in Portland?
> **What time** are we boarding?

If you want to ask how much time something takes, use **How long ... ?**

> **How long** is the flight?
> **How long** does the trip take?
> **How long** does it take?
> **How long** will it take us to walk there?

Useful words

a bus	a large motor vehicle that carries passengers
downtown	in or toward the center of a city
a platform	the area in a train station where you wait for a train
far	a long way from somewhere
the right	the side that is towards the east when you look north
board	to get into a train, a ship, or an aircraft to travel somewhere

If you want to ask how many times something happens, use **How often do ... ?**

> **How often do** the trains leave?
> **How often do** the trains to Cambridge leave?
> **How often do** the buses to Edinburgh leave?

If you want to ask about the money that you need to do something, use **How much ... ?**

> **How much** is a ticket to Beijing?
> **How much** is a round-trip ticket?
> **How much** does it cost to fly there?
> **How much** does it cost to rent a car?

Use **Can I ... ?** to ask if you are allowed to do something.

> **Can I** buy a ticket on the train?
> **Can I** leave my bags here?
> **Can I** change my ticket if I need to?
> **Can I** pay by credit card?

Asking for things

To ask for something, use **Can I have ... ?** or **Could I have ... ?** To be very polite, add **please** to the question.

> **Can I have** a train timetable, please?
> **Can I have** a ticket to Wellington, please?

> **Could I have** two seats together, please?
> **Could I have** a round-trip ticket to San Francisco, please?

Useful words

a round-trip ticket	a ticket for a journey to a place and back again
a credit card	a plastic card that you use to buy something and pay for it later
a timetable	a list of the times when trains, buses, or planes arrive and depart
a seat	something that you can sit on

You can also ask for something by using **I'd like ...** . Again, to be very polite, add **please** to the end of the sentence.

>**I'd like** two seats, please.
>**I'd like** a receipt, please.
>**I'd like** an aisle seat, please

If you want to find out if something is available, use **Do you have ... ?**

>**Do you have** a map of the city?
>**Do you have** any smaller cars to rent?
>Excuse me, **do you have** any bus timetables?

If you are asking someone if they can do something for you, you should use **Can you ... ?** or **Could you ... ? Could you ... ?** is slightly more polite and formal than **Can you ... ?** To be polite, you can add **please** to the questions.

>**Can you** take us to the Saint-Antoine Hotel, **please**?
>**Can you** stop here, **please**?
>**Can you** please show us where it is on the map?

>**Could you** write down the address for me, **please**?
>**Could you** show us where it is?
>**Could you** give me the number, **please**?
>**Could you** give us directions, **please**?

Useful words

a receipt	a piece of paper that shows that you have received goods or money
an aisle	a long, narrow passage where people can walk between rows of seats
a map	a drawing of a particular area, such as a city or a country, that shows things like mountains, rivers, and roads
an address	the number of the building, the name of the street, and the town or city where you live or work
directions	instructions that tell you how to get somewhere

When you ask for something, you can simply name what you want, making sure you finish the sentence with **please**.

> **A** one-way ticket to Lima, **please**.
> **A** subway map, **please**.
> **A** window seat, **please**.
> **Three** round-trip tickets to Montreal, **please**.
> **Two** travel passes, **please**.

Saying what you like, dislike, prefer

You may want to talk about what you like and do not like about traveling. To say what you like, use **I like …** . To say what you do not like, use **I don't like …** .

> **I like** these country roads.
> **I like** traveling by train.
> **I like** seeing a different way of life.
> I really **like** to be in the mountains with all the snow.

> **I don't like** flying.
> **I don't like** to drive on the right.
> **I don't like** being away from my family and friends.
> I like the country very much, but **I don't like** the heat.

Useful words

a one-way ticket	a ticket that you use to travel to a place but not return from it
the subway	a railway system that runs under the ground
a window	a space in the wall of a building or in the side of a vehicle that has glass in it
country	land that is away from cities and towns
a way of life	the things that people normally do in a place
snow	soft, white frozen water that falls from the sky
right	the side that is toward the east when you look north
the heat	when something is hot

> **GOOD TO KNOW!**
> **like + -ing**
> When **like ...** is followed by a verb, the verb can be in the -ing or infinitive (to + verb) form.

To ask what someone else likes, use **Do you like ... ?**

Do you like this area?
Do you like traveling by yourself?
Do you like to drive at night?

If you want to say that you like something very much, use **I really like ...** or **I love ...** .

I really like camping.
I really like to visit other countries.
I really like trains.

I love to hike in the hills in that region.
I love driving through the countryside.
We love all the lakes.

If you want to say that you like one thing more than another thing, use **I prefer ...** .

I prefer staying in hotels.
I prefer to take the highway.
I prefer driving in the daytime when I can see all the scenery.
I do travel on my own, but **I prefer** traveling with other people.

Useful words

an area	a particular part of a town, a country, a region, or the world
by yourself	on your own and not with anyone else
camping	staying somewhere in a tent
a hill	an area of land that is higher than the land around it
a region	an area of the country or of the world
a lake	a large area of water with land around it
a highway	a main road that connects towns or cities
the daytime	the part of the day between the time when it gets light and the time when it gets dark
scenery	the land, water, or plants that you can see around you in a country area

● Listen for

Here are some important phrases you are likely to hear and use when you are traveling.

Tickets, please.
Could I see your tickets, please?
Have your tickets ready, please.
Next stop ....
This is the 5:45 to London, stopping at Finsbury Park only.
A round-trip ticket to Portland, please.
A one-way ticket to Seoul, please.
You need to change at Times Square.
The train for Vancouver leaves from Platform Three.
Do you mind if I sit here?
Go straight until you get to the traffic light.
Continue on this road.
Take the second turn on the left.
It's opposite the cathedral.
It's very near.
You can walk there.
It's too far to walk.
It'll take you ten minutes to walk there.
It's three stops from here.

Useful words	
ready	prepared
Do you mind ... ?	used to ask someone if you can do something
straight on	continuing in one direction
continue	start again after stopping
opposite	across from

Listen to the conversation: Track 3

Scott is in the ticket office of a train station, buying his ticket.

A I'd like a one-way ticket to New Haven, please. I need to be there by noon.

B Right, you need the 8:35 train. That will be $110.00.

A Thank you.

B You have to change at Penn Station.

A Ok. What time does the train arrive in New Haven?

B 11:32.

A Uh-huh. Which platform does the train leave from?

B Platform 18.

A Where's Platform 18?

B It's at the far end of the station.

A Ok, thanks.

Katie and Emma are starting to plan a vacation together.

A I like the sun, so I want to go somewhere nice and hot.

B Me, too. We could go to New Mexico. I've never been there, but it sounds great.

A I love New Mexico. Let's look online and see what we can find.

B Good idea. The only thing is... I really don't want to fly.

A What about driving? We could even rent a car and share the driving between us.

B That would be great. Maybe we could stop off at the Grand Canyon. I've always wanted to go there.

A Let's see if we have time. Remember, I have to be back here by the beginning of September.

B Oh yes, that's when school starts, isn't it?

A Yes, but that still leaves us three weeks.

B That should be plenty of time!

 Listen to more phrases and practice saying them: Track 4

Where we live

Make yourself at home!

The phrases in this unit will help you to talk about places to live or to stay when you are away from home. You can use them if you are trying to find a hotel, if you are looking for somewhere to live, or if you want to talk about the place where you live.

Asking for things

To say what you want, use **I'd like ...** .

> **I'd like** a double room.
> **I'd like** to stay three nights.
> **I'd like** an apartment near the university.
> **I'd like** a room with a private bathroom.

To talk about the kind of place you want to stay or live, use **I'm looking for ...** .

> **I'm looking for** a hotel downtown.
> **I'm looking for** cheap accommodations in the area.
> **I'm looking for** a place to rent.
> **We're looking for** a house with four bedrooms.

GOOD TO KNOW!
Accommodations has an unusual spelling. Remember that it has **cc** and **mm**.

Useful words

a double room	a room for two people
an apartment	a group of rooms where someone lives in a large building
private	only for one particular person or group, and not for everyone
accommodations	buildings or rooms where people live or stay
rent	to pay the owner of something in order to be able to use it yourself

To explain to someone what you want, use **I want ...** .

> **I want** a house with a large garden.
> **I want** to rent a house for six months.
> **I want** a room with a view of the ocean.

If you are in a hotel and you need something, use **Could I have ... ?**

> **Could I have** the key to my room, please?
> **Could I have** a receipt, please?
> **Could I have** two more towels?

To make sure that a hotel has everything you need, use **Do you have ... ?**

> **Do you have** Internet access?
> **Do you have** a gym?
> **Do you have** any rooms available?

To ask someone to do something for you, use **Could you ... ?**

> **Could you** show me the room, please?
> **Could you** get someone to fix the window?
> **Could you** call a taxi for me, please?

Useful words

a garden	the part of a yard where you grow flowers and vegetables
the view	everything that you can see from a place
a receipt	a piece of paper that shows that you have paid for something
a towel	a piece of thick soft cloth that you use to dry yourself
access	when you are able to use equipment
a gym	a building or a large room with equipment for doing physical exercises
available	that you can find or get
fix	if you fix something, you repair it

Talking about yourself

When you are looking for somewhere to live or stay, you may have to talk about yourself. To say what your name is, use **I'm ...** or **My name's ...** .

> **I'm** Grace.
> Hi, **I'm** Barbara. I'm here to look at the room.

> **My name's** Alejandro Perez. I have a reservation for tonight.
> Hello, **my name's** Megan Keane. I'd like to speak to a real estate agent, please.

To give general information about yourself, use **I'm ...** .

> **I'm** French, but I'm studying here.
> **I'm** very neat.
> **I'm** the owner of the apartment, but I don't live here.

To talk about your work, use **I'm a ...** with the name of a job, or **I work ...** to say something more general about what you do.

> **I'm a** student.
> **I'm a** teacher.

> **I work** at the airport.
> **I work** for a trucking company.
> **I work** as a translator.

Useful words

make a reservation	to ask a hotel or a restaurant to keep a room or a table for you
a real estate agent	a person whose job is to sell buildings or land
neat	liking everything to be in its correct place
a translator	someone whose job is to say or write things in a different language

Asking for information

A simple way to ask for information about places to stay or live, is to start your sentence with **Is ... ?**

> **Is** it expensive?
> **Is** it far from the center of town?
> **Is** breakfast included in the price?

To ask if a place has something, use **Is there ... ?** or **Are there any ... ?**

> **Is there** a hair dryer in the room?
> **Is there** a TV?
> **Is there** a pool?

> **Are there any** good schools near here?
> **Are there any** rules about having guests?
> **Are there any** more blankets?

You could also use **Does ... have ... ?**

> **Does** the apartment **have** central heating?
> **Does** the hotel **have** a swimming pool?
> **Does** it **have** a garden?
> **Does** it **have** a parking lot?

Useful words	
expensive	costing a lot of money
include	to have something as one part
a hair dryer	a machine that you use to dry your hair
a guest	someone who you invite to your home
a blanket	a large, thick piece of cloth that you put on a bed to keep you warm
central heating	a heating system that uses hot air or water to heat every part of a building
a parking lot	an area of ground where people can leave their cars

You can ask questions using **What ... ?** or **Where ... ?**

> **What**'s the name of the hotel?
> **What**'s the average price of an apartment in this area?
> **What**'s the landlord's address?

> **Where**'s the closest restaurant?
> **Where** is the best gym?
> **Where** are the elevators?

To ask about time, use **What time ... ?**

> **What time**'s dinner?
> **What time** do you lock the doors at night?
> **What time** do we have to leave in the morning?

To ask about prices, use **How much ... ?**

> **How much** is a double room?
> **How much** is the rent?
> **How much** do you charge for Internet service?

Useful words

average	the normal amount for a particular group
a landlord	a man who owns a building and allows people to live there in return for rent
an elevator	a machine that carries people or things up and down in tall buildings
lock	to close a door or a container with a key
rent	the money you pay to the owner of something to be able to use it yourself
charge	to ask someone to pay money for something

Asking if something is allowed or permitted

If you are staying in a hotel or renting a place to live, you may need to ask if something is allowed. You can use **Can I ... ?**

> **Can I** see the room?
> **Can I** pay by credit card?
> **Can we** use the pool?
> **Can we** camp here?

To check if you can do something, use **Is it OK to ... ?**

> **Is it OK to** use the washing machine?
> **Is it OK to** have guests?
> **Is it OK to** bring our dog?

To make sure you will not upset someone, use **Do you mind if ... ?**

> **Do you mind if** I park my car here for a moment?
> **Do you mind if** leave my suitcase here for five minutes?
> **Do you mind if** we look at the rooms before we decide?

You can also use **Is it OK to ... ?** This is slightly informal.

> **Is it OK to** use the stove?
> **Is it OK to** play my guitar?
> **Is it OK to** have guests?

Useful words

a credit card	a plastic card that you use to buy something and pay for it later
a pool	a place where people can swim
camp	to stay somewhere in a tent
a washing machine	a machine that you use to wash clothes in
a suitcase	a case for carrying your clothes when you are traveling
a stove	a piece of kitchen equipment that is used for cooking food
a guitar	a musical instrument with strings

Saying what you like, dislike, prefer

To talk about what you like, use **I like ...** .

> **I like** small hotels.
> **I like** campsites in the mountains.
> **I like** this part of the city.

If you like something very much, use **I really like ...** or **I love ...** .

> **I really like** living here.
> **I really like** your sofa.
> **I really like** being so close to my work.

> **I love** modern furniture.
> **I love** the peace of the countryside.
> **I love** living on my own.

> **GOOD TO KNOW!**
> **Like/Love + -ing**
> When **like** or **love** is followed by a verb, the verb is often in the -ing form.

If you do not like something, use **I don't like ...** .

> **I don't like** this hotel.
> **I don't like** living with my brother.
> **I don't like** this building.

Useful words

a campsite	a place where you can stay in a tent
a sofa	a long, comfortable seat with a back, and usually with arms, that two or three people can sit on
peace	the state of being quiet and calm
countryside	land that is away from cities and towns

If you want to say that you like one thing more than another, use **I prefer**. If you want to talk about the thing you like less, use **to**.

> **I prefer** living near the beach **to** living in the city.
> **I prefer** living alone.
> **I prefer** this town **to** my hometown.

Talking about your plans

When you are talking about your plans for where you're going to live or stay, use **I'm going to ...** .

> **I'm going to** stay in Vail.
> **I'm going to** rent a cabin in the mountains.
> **We're going to** go camping.

You can also use **I'll** plus a verb in the simple form [the infinitive is the verb + "to"].

> **I'll be** staying for a week.
> **I'll pay** the rent in advance.
> **We'll arrive** in the evening.

You can tell people about your plans using **I'm planning to ...** .

> **I'm planning to** buy an apartment near the river.
> **I'm planning to** rent a room in a colleague's house.
> **I'm planning to** move to Daejon.

Useful words

a cabin	a small wooden house in the woods or mountains
in advance	before a particular date or event
a colleague	a person someone works with
move	to go to live in a different place

Complaining

You may need to complain about the place where you are staying or living. A simple way to start a sentence explaining what is wrong is to use **It's ...** .

> **It's** very cold in my room.
> **It's** too expensive.
> **It's** not big enough.

To talk about something that should not be in the place where you are living or staying, use **There's ...** .

> **There's** too much noise.
> **There's** dirt all over the floor.
> **There's** a hole in the wall.

If you think you should have something that you do not have, use **There isn't ...** .

> **There isn't** any hot water.
> **There isn't** anyplace to keep my bike.
> **There isn't** enough room for all my books.

If something is not good enough, use **I'm not happy with ...** .

> **I'm not happy with** the food.
> **I'm not happy with** my room.
> **I'm not happy with** the way the place is cleaned.

Useful words
a hole   an opening or an empty space in something

● Listen for

Here are some useful phrases you may hear when you are looking for a place to stay or live.

> What type of accommodations are you looking for?
> Whose name is the reservation in?
> For how many nights?
> For how many people?
> Breakfast is included.
> Can I see your passport, please?
> I'm sorry. We're full.
> There's a 300 dollar deposit.
> What number can we contact you at?
> We don't allow dogs.
> How would you like to pay?
> Please fill out this form.
> Please sign here.
> Can you spell your name for me, please?

Useful words

a deposit	a sum of money that is part of the full price of something, and that you pay when you agree to buy it
contact	to telephone someone or send them a message or letter
fill something out	to write information in the spaces on a form
a form	a piece of paper with questions on it and spaces where you should write the answers
sign	to write your name on a document
spell	to write or speak each letter of a word in the correct order

Listen to the conversation: Track 5

It's Scott's first day at his new job at an IT company in Ann Arbor. He's having coffee with his new colleague Laura.

A I hope you're enjoying living in Ann Arbor, Scott. It's a great city. Have you found a place to live yet?

B No, I'm staying in a hotel at the moment, but I'd like to find a room in a house.

A Wouldn't you prefer to live alone?

B No, I thought it'd be a good way to make friends, at least at first.

A Well, actually, there is a room available in the house where I live. It's a big house — there are five of us there. You could come and look at it if you like.

B Thanks very much. What's the house like? Does it have central heating? I've heard the winters here are really cold!

A Oh, yes, don't worry — it's a modern house, and it's very warm and comfortable.

B Are there any rules about having guests? My brother will probably come to visit this summer.

A That's fine — we all have guests sometimes. It's a very friendly house. I really like living there.

B Could I see the room this evening?

A Sure, I'll give you the address.

 Listen to more phrases and practice saying them: Track 6

Eating with friends

Enjoy your meal!

If you are going out for a meal, you will need to make arrangements with your friends about when and where to meet. You will also want to order food and perhaps tell your friends what food you like and do not like. The phrases in this unit will help you to do all this with confidence.

Making arrangements

To suggest a plan to a friend, use **We can ...** .

> **We can** have coffee somewhere.
> **We can** have dinner in town.
> **We can** have lunch together sometime.
> **We can** eat out.

To say that you will do something as part of that plan, use **I'll ...** .

> **I'll** meet you at the café.
> **I'll** meet you outside the restaurant.
> **I'll** be inside the restaurant.
> **I'll** get to the restaurant by seven o'clock.

To ask someone about the place they want to meet, use **Where ... ?**

> **Where** should we meet?
> **Where** do you want to eat?
> **Where** would you like to eat?

Useful words

a meal	an occasion when people sit down and eat
order	to ask for food and drinks to be brought to you in a restaurant
dinner	the main meal of the day, usually served in the evening
lunch	the meal that you have in the middle of the day
eat out	to eat in a restaurant

To ask someone about the time they want to meet, use **When ... ?** or **What time ... ?**

> **When** should we eat?
> **When** do you want to meet for dinner?
> **When** do you want to have dinner?

> **What time** should we meet?
> **What time** would you like to meet?
> **What time** would you like to eat?

To make sure someone is happy with a plan, use **Is ... OK?**

> **Is** seven o'clock **OK**?
> **Is** Italian **OK** with you?
> **Is** it **OK** to come a little later?
> **Is** it **OK** to meet inside the restaurant?

To ask what the best plan is, use **Is it better to ... ?**

> **Is it better to** meet outside the restaurant?
> **Is it better to** make a reservation?
> **Is it better to** arrive early?
> **Is it better to** go to a restaurant that we?

Asking for information

To ask about the place where you're going, use **Where is ... ?**

> **Where is** the restaurant?
> Excuse me, **where are** the menus?

Useful words

late	after the time that something should start or happen
make a reservation	to ask a hotel or a restaurant to keep a room or a table for you
early	before the usual time

To ask about the price of something, use **How much ... ?**

> **How much** is a bottle of water?
> **How much** is it for a pizza?
> **How much** is the beef stew?

Use **What is ... ?** to ask about a particular dish.

> **What is** "gravy"?
> Excuse me, **what is** "jelly"?

Use **What is in ... ?** to ask about the food in a particular dish.

> **What is in** this dish?
> **What's in** the stew?

Use **Is there any ... ?** or **Are there any ... ?** to ask whether a particular food is in a dish.

> **Is there any** milk in this dessert?
> **Are there any** nuts in this?

Useful words	
a dish	food that is prepared in a particular way
gravy	a sauce made from the juices that come from meat when it cooks
jelly	a sweet food that contains soft fruit and sugar
stew	a meal that you make by cooking meat and vegetables in a liquid
a dessert	something sweet that you eat at the end of a meal
a nut	a dry fruit with a hard shell

Asking for things

When you arrive at the restaurant, you will want to tell the waiter or waitress how many people will be eating so she can find the right sized table for you. Use **A table for ... please**.

> **A table for** two, **please**.
> "**A table for** six, **please**." "Certainly, sir."

In most restaurants, someone will soon come to your table to take your order. To say which dish you want, use **I'd like ...** or **I'll have ...** . To be very polite, use **please** after this.

> **I'd like** a sausage pizza, please.
> **I'd like** the pizza too, please.
> For an appetizer, **I'd like** the salad, please.
> For my main course, **I'd like** the pasta.
> For dessert, **I'd like** ice cream.

> **I'll have** the lamb, please.
> **I'll have** the salad as an appetizer, please.
> For my main course, **I'll have** the fish soup.
> For dessert, **I'll have** the fruit.
> **We'll have** water to drink.

> **GOOD TO KNOW!**
> If the waiter or waitress comes to your table to take your order, and you have not decided what to choose, say **We haven't decided yet** or **Could you come back in a few minutes, please?**

Useful words

a waiter	a man whose job is to serve food in a restaurant
a waitress	a woman whose job is to serve food in a restaurant
an appetizer	a small amount of food that you eat as the first part of a meal
a salad	a mixture of food, usually vegetables, that you usually serve cold
a main course	the biggest part of a meal
pasta	a type of food made from a mixture of flour, eggs and water that is made into different shapes and then boiled
a soup	a liquid food made by boiling meat, fish, or vegetables in water

To ask if something is available, use **Do you have ... ?**

> **Do you have** a children's menu?
> **Do you have** a table outside?

If the waiter or waitress has brought food to your table but you need something else, use **Can I have ... ?** or **Could I have ... ?** To be very polite, use **please**.

> **Can I have** some more bread, please?
> Please **can I have** the dessert menu?
> **Can I have** some pepper, please?
> **Can I have** some ketchup, please?

> **Could I have** another fork, please?
> Please **could I have** some water?
> **Could we have** a bigger table, please?
> **Could I have** the bill, please?

If you are asking someone if they can do something for you, use **Can you ... ?** or **Could you ... ? Could you ... ?** is slightly more polite and formal than **Can you ... ?** To be very polite, use **please**.

> **Can you** pass me the salt, please?
> **Can you** close the window, please?
> **Can you** bring another glass, please?
> **Can you** please bring us some more water?

Useful words

a menu	a list of the food and drinks that you can have in a restaurant
outside	not in a building but very close to it
pepper	a spice with a hot taste that you put on food
ketchup	a thick red sauce made from tomatoes
a fork	a tool with long metal points used for eating food
the bill	a piece of paper that shows how much money you must pay for something
pass	to give an object to someone
salt	a white substance that you use to improve the flavor of food

Could you take our order, please?
Could you bring us our coffee, please?
Could you bring us the bill, please?
Could you clear the table, please?

Saying what you want to do

To say what you want to do, use **I'd like to ...** .

I'd like to make a reservation, please.
I'd like to try that new Spanish restaurant on Green Street.
I'd like to see the dessert menu.
We'd like to order dessert, please.
We'd like to pay by credit card.

Saying what you like, dislike, prefer

When you are eating in a restaurant, you may want to talk about the food that you like and don't like. To talk about food that you like, use **I like ...** and to ask someone if they like something, use **Do you like ... ?**

I like cheese.
I like all vegetables.

Do you like fish?
Do you like spicy food?
Do you like Thai food?

Useful words

an order	the thing that someone has asked for
a plate	a flat dish that is used for holding food
a credit card	a small piece of plastic that you use to pay for things
cheese	a solid yellow or white food made from milk
a vegetable	a plant that you can cook and eat
spicy	strongly flavored with spices

If you like something, but not in a strong way, use **I sort of like ...** .

> **I sort of like** ice cream.
> **I sort of like** burgers.

If you like something very much, you can say **I really like ...** or **I love ...** .

> **I really like** Japanese food.
> **I really like** meat.

> **I love** seafood.
> **I love** dessert.

To tell someone that you do not like a food, use **I don't like ...** .

> **I don't like** olives.
> **I don't like** hot food.
> **I don't like** fast food.

To confirm that something is true, use **Don't you ... ?**

> **Don't you like** sweet food?
> **Don't you like** chocolate?

Useful words

meat	the part of an animal that people cook and eat
seafood	fish and other small animals from the sea that you can eat
an olive	a small green or black fruit with a bitter taste
hot	having a strong, burning taste
fast food	hot food that is served quickly in a restaurant
sweet	containing a lot of sugar
chocolate	a sweet brown food made from cocoa

To say very strongly that you do not like a food, use **I hate...** .

> **I hate** mushrooms.
> **She hates** tomatoes.
> **I hate** that flavor.

If you want to say that you like one food more than another, use **I prefer...** .
If you want to talk about the food you like less, use **to** before it.

> I don't really like meat. **I prefer** fish.
> **I prefer** eating at home **to** eating at a restaurant.

Asking for suggestions

If you want to ask the waiter or the people at your table to suggest something to eat, use **What do you recommend ... ?**

> **What do you recommend** for an appetizer?
> **What do you recommend** for dessert?
> You've been to this restaurant before, Pilar. **What do you recommend**?

To give you an idea about what to eat, you might ask someone at your table what they have chosen. Use **What are you having ... ?**

> **What are you having**, Juan?
> **What are you having** for dessert, Yuta?
> **What are you having** for your appetizer?

Useful words

a mushroom	a plant with a short stem and a round part that you can eat
a tomato	a soft red fruit that you can eat raw in salads or cook like a vegetable
a flavor	the taste of a food or drink

If you want to ask whether you should have or do something, use **Do you think I should ... ?**

> **Do you think I should** have the pie?
> **Do you think I should** try the snails?
> **Do you think we should** leave a larger tip?

Making suggestions

One easy way of making suggestions about where to eat and what to eat is to use **We could ...** .

> **We could** eat here, if you like.
> **We could** have coffee with our dessert.
> **We could** just have a salad.

If you are eager to do something, use **Let's ...** .

> **Let's** order a pizza.
> **Let's** ask Neil to join us for dinner.
> **Let's** try that new French restaurant.

If you want to make a suggestion and see if other people agree with you, use **Should we ... ?**

> **Should we** eat now?
> **Should we** order?
> **Should we** wait till Maria comes to order?

Useful words	
a pie	a dish of fruit, meat, or vegetables that is covered with pastry (= a mixture of flour, butter, and water) and baked
a snail	a small animal with a long, soft body, no legs, and a shell on its back
a tip	money that you give to someone to thank them for a job that they have done for you
join	to come together with other people

If you have an idea about something, use **How about ... ?**

> **How about** finding somewhere in town to eat?
> **How about** sitting outside to eat?
> **How about** sharing a dessert?

> **GOOD TO KNOW!**
> **How about + -ing**
> The verb that comes after **How about** must be in the -ing form.

Talking about your plans

To say what you have decided to eat, use **I'm having the ...** or **I'm going to have the ...** .

> **I'm having the** pie.
> **I'm having the** soup for an appetizer.

> **I'm going to have the** fish stew.
> **I'm going to have the** pasta for my main course.

If you do not know what to choose, use **I can't decide what to have ...** .

> **I can't decide what to have** for an appetizer.
> **I can't decide what to have** for a main course.
> There are so many delicious things. **I can't decide what to have**.

If you think you might choose something, use **Maybe I'll have the ...** .

> **Maybe I'll have the** salad for my appetizer.
> **Maybe I'll have the** salmon for my main course.

Useful words

share	to have or use something with another person
delicious	very good to eat
salmon	the pink flesh of a large fish with silver skin

● Listen for

Here are some useful phrases you may hear in a restaurant.

Do you have a reservation?
I'm sorry. We're full.
This way, please.
Follow me, please.
Smoking or non-smoking?
Here's the menu.
Are you ready to order?
Can I take your order?
And for you, Sir?
And for you, Madam?
Today's specials are on the board.
I'd recommend the fish tacos.
The pasta comes with a green salad.
Would you like to start with an appetizer?
What will you have to drink?
Would you like anything else?
Can I get you anything else?
Is everything all right?
I'll be right with you.
I'll bring it right away.

Useful words

full	containing as many people as possible
a special	a dish in a restaurant that is available only on a particular day and is not usually available
a board	a flat piece of wood that you use for a special purpose
taco	a crispy Mexican pancake made from corn and eggs, which is folded and filled with meat, vegetables, and a spicy sauce.
right away	immediately

Listen to the conversation: Track 7

Laura and Scott are in a restaurant. They're deciding what to eat.

A There's a lot of fish on the menu. Do you like fish?

B I like it a lot, but I really prefer meat to fish.

A I really like fish – I'm going to have the salmon.

B I can't decide what to have.

A How about the lamb? That sounds good.

B I think it sounds spicy. I hate spicy food.

A We could go somewhere else if you prefer.

B No, I'm sure I'll find something I like. Maybe I'll have the pasta. Oh, never mind — the pasta has olives in it.

A Don't you like olives?

B Not really.

A I love them. I eat them all the time.

B You've eaten in this restaurant a few times, haven't you?

A Sure.

B Well, what do you recommend?

A They make really good pizza. Why not have pizza?

B That's a good idea.

A   So, are you ready to order?

B   Yes, let's call our waiter over.

 Listen to more phrases and practice saying them: Track 8

Going out

Have a good time!

If you are going out, whether it is to a party, a concert, or the movies, these phrases will help you say what you want, ask where things are, and ask for what you need.

Making suggestions

One easy way of making a suggestion about where to go and what to do, is to use **We could ...** .

> **We could** go to the park, if you like.
> **We could** go to the theater, if you want.
> **We could** see a movie.

> **GOOD TO KNOW!**
> When people start a sentence with **We could,** they often add **if you like**.

If you are eager to do something with someone, use **Let's ...** .

> **Let's** go to the movies.
> **Let's** buy tickets for Saturday's game.
> I've got a good idea! **Let's** go swimming.

Useful words	
a park	a public area of land with grass and trees, usually in a town, where people go to relax and enjoy themselves
the theater	the place where you go to see plays or shows
a movie	a story that is told in a series of moving pictures
a ticket	a small piece of paper that shows that you have paid to go somewhere or do something
a game	an activity or a sport in which you try to win against someone
swimming	the activity of moving through water by making movements with your arms and legs

Another way to make a suggestion about where to go and what to do is to use **Should we ... ?**

> **Should we** go out for dinner?
> **Should we** go to a café?
> **Should we** go for a walk?

If you have an idea about what to do or where to go, use **How about ... ?**

> **How about** going somewhere for coffee?
> **How about** going bowling?
> **How about** going on a picnic?

> **GOOD TO KNOW!**
> **How about + -ing**
> The verb that comes after **How about** must be in the -ing form.

To suggest what someone else can do or where someone else can go, use **You could ... .**

> **You could** go to a concert.
> **You could** have ice cream on the deck.
> **You could** go to a soccer game.

Useful words

bowling	a game in which you roll a heavy ball down a narrow track toward a group of wooden objects and try to knock them down
a picnic	a meal that is eaten outdoors
a concert	a performance of music
a deck	a flat wooden area attached to a house, where people can sit
a game	an activity or a sport in which you try to win against someone

You can also use **Why not ... ?** if you have an idea about what someone else might do.

> **Why not** go to Helena's party?
> **Why not** have a party for him.
> **Why not** invite some friends from work?

Talking about your plans

For a plan that you are sure of, use **I'm going to ...** . Use **Are you going to ... ?** to ask someone about their plan.

> **I'm going to** have a party.
> **I'm going to** go out with some friends tonight.
> **We're going to** have dinner at our friends' house tonight.

> **Are you going to** celebrate?
> **Are you going to** see Ava tonight?
> **Are you going to** invite many people?

You can also use **Will you ... ?** to ask if someone is going to do something.

> **Will you** take a taxi home after the concert?
> **Will you** buy the tickets?
> **Will you** call the box office or should I?

Useful words

a party	a social event often to celebrate something
invite	to ask someone to come to an event
celebrate	to do something enjoyable for a special reason
a taxi	a car with a driver who you pay to take you somewhere
the box office	the place in a theater where the tickets are sold

To talk about something that you would like to do but are not sure that you will do, you can use **I hope to ...** .

> **I hope to** see them in concert.
> **I hope to** visit Marrakech while I'm in Morocco.
> **We hope to** go to the ballet while we're in Moscow.

To talk about a plan that is possible but not certain, use **I might ...** .

> **I might** see a band this weekend.
> **I might** meet up with Farida and Saki tonight.
> **We might** go to a café afterwards.

Asking for information

Use **Is there ... ?** or **Are there ... ?** to ask if something exists where you are. You may need to get someone's attention before you can ask them this question. Use **Excuse me** to do this.

> Excuse me, **is there** a café near here?
> Excuse me, **is there** a bookstore in this part of town?
> **Is there** a football game this afternoon?

> Excuse me, **are there** any parks in this area?
> Excuse me, **are there** any free concerts this weekend?
> **Are there** any clubs near here?

Useful words

ballet	a type of dancing that needs a lot of skill and in which there are carefully planned movements
a band	a group of people who play music together
meet up	to come together with people
free	used for describing things that you do not have to pay for

If you are looking for something, and you want information about how to find it, use **Where ... ?**

> **Where** is the Belgrade Theater?
> **Where** is the Arts Cinema?
> **Where** can I buy a ticket for the game?

If you want to know the time that something happens, use **What time ... ?**

> **What time** does the movie start?
> **What time** does the concert finish?
> **What time** should we meet?

To ask how much time something lasts, use **How long ... ?**

> **How long** is the movie?
> **How long** is the concert?
> **How long** will you be there?

If you want to ask about the money that you need to do something, use **How much ... ?**

> **How much** is it to get in?
> **How much** is a ticket?
> **How much** does it cost?

To ask someone whether something is available, use **Do you have ... ?**

> **Do you have** any tickets left?
> **Do you have** any tickets for tonight's performance?
> **Do you have** any programs?

Useful words

a game	an activity or a sport in which you try to win against someone
get in	to enter somewhere
left	still there after everything else has gone or been used
a performance	when you entertain an audience by singing, dancing or acting
a program	a small book or sheet of paper that tells you about a play or concert

Asking for things

To ask for something, use **Can I have ... ?** or **Could I have ... ?** To be very polite, use **please**.

> **Can I have** two tickets for the show, please?
> **Can I have** a concert program, please?
>
> **Could I have** a cup of coffee, please?
> **Could I have** some more?

Another way of asking for something is **I'd like ...** .

> **I'd like** a glass of orange juice, please.
> **I'd like** a ticket for tonight's game.
> **I'd like** three tickets, please.

If you are asking someone if they can do something for you, use **Can you ... ?** or **Could you ... ? Could you ... ?** is slightly more polite and formal than **Can you ... ?** To be polite, use **please**.

> **Can you** tell me where the entrance is, please?
> **Could you** take me to Times Square, please?

Useful words

show	a performance in a theater
an orange	a round, juicy fruit with a thick, orange-colored skin
juice	the liquid from a fruit or a vegetable
entrance	the door or gate where you go into a place

Saying what you like, dislike, prefer

To talk about things you like, use **I like ...** and to ask someone if they like something, use **Do you like ... ?**

> **I like** listening to live music.
> **I like** going out with my friends.
> **He likes** dance music.

> **Do you like** dancing?
> **Do you like** horror movies?
> **Do you like** eating out?

> **GOOD TO KNOW!**
> **like + -ing**
> When **like** is followed by a verb, the verb is usually in the -ing form.

If you like something, but not in a strong way, use **I like ...** .

> **I like** going to the movies.
> **I like** the theater.

If you like something very much, you can say **I really like ...** or **I love ...** .

> **I really like** going on picnics in the summer.
> **I really like** going to the opera.

> **I love** musicals.
> **I love** having dinner with my friends.
> **I love** walking home on nice days.

Useful words

dancing	the activity of moving your body to music
a horror movie	a very frightening movie that you watch for entertainment
eat out	to eat in a restaurant
an opera	a play in which the words are sung
a musical	a play or a movie that uses singing or dancing in the story

To tell someone what you do not like, use **I don't like ...** .

> **I don't like** football.
> **I don't like** going to the theater.
> **I don't** really **like** science fiction movies.

To say very strongly that you do not like something, use **I hate ...** .

> **I hate** the opera.
> **I hate** being in a crowd.
> I absolutely **hate** noisy clubs.

> **GOOD TO KNOW!**
> **Hate + -ing**
> When **hate** is followed by a verb, the verb is usually in the -ing form.

If you want to say that you like one thing more than another, use **I prefer ...** .
If you want to talk about the thing you like less, use **to**.

> **I prefer** going to the movies **to** watching DVDs at home.
> **I prefer** having dinner at home **to** eating out.

Expressing opinions

Use **I thought ...** to give your opinion of a movie you have seen, a concert you have been to, or something else that you have done.

> **I thought** it was a really good movie.
> **I thought** the play was a little long.
> **I thought** it was an excellent concert.

Useful words

science fiction	stories about life in the future or in other parts of the universe
a crowd	a large group of people who have gathered together
noisy	making a lot of loud or unpleasant noise
excellent	extremely good

If you want to ask other people if they think something is good or bad, use **What did you think of ... ?**

>**What did you think of** the band?
>**What did you think of** her voice?
>**What did you think of** the meal?

You can also ask someone for their opinion by saying **What's your opinion of ... ?**

>**What's your opinion of** her latest movie?
>**What's your opinion of** the new club that opened on Kerbey Lane?

To agree with someone's opinion, use **I agree**. If you want to say who you agree with, use **with**.

>"This is a really cool nightclub." "**I agree**."
>**I agree with** Francine. It's a fantastic restaurant.
>I completely **agree with** you. It was a terrible game.

You can also use **You're right ...** to agree with what someone has said.

>"**You're right**. She can't sing!"
>I think **you're right**. His first movie was much better.
>Luca**'s right**. The food here is great.

Useful words

your voice	the sound that comes out from your mouth when you speak or sing
a meal	the food that you have on one occasion
cool	fashionable and interesting
a nightclub	a place where people go late in the evening to dance
fantastic	very good
terrible	very bad
sing	to make music with your voice

If you do not agree with someone, you can use **I disagree**. If you want to say who you disagree with, use **with**.

> "I think the nightlife in the city has really improved." "I'm afraid **I disagree**."
> I'm afraid **I disagree with** you.
> **I disagree with** Martin. There's not much for young people to do in the evening.

> **GOOD TO KNOW!**
> When people say **I disagree,** they often use **I'm afraid** to be very polite.

You can also use **I don't think so** to disagree with someone.

> "The show is too long." "**I don't think so**. I enjoyed it from beginning to end."
> "That restaurant has really improved." "**I don't think so**. I had a really bad meal there a month ago."
> "It's the best club in town." "**I don't think so**. I much prefer Dino's."

Asking if something is allowed or permitted

If you need to ask if you can do something when you are out, the simplest way is to use **Can I ... ?**

> **Can I** sit anywhere?
> **Can I** pay by credit card?
> **Can I** take this chair?
> **Can we** sit outside?

Useful words
nightlife   entertainment at night, for example nightclubs
improve   to get better

If you want to make sure that someone will not be unhappy or angry if you do something, use **Do you mind if ... ?**

> **Do you mind if** I get to the restaurant a little late?
> **Do you mind if** I join you?
> **Do you mind if** we sit here?

You can also use **Is it OK ... ?** This is slightly informal, but you can use it in most situations.

> **Is it OK** to take my cell in with me?
> **Is it OK** to leave my bag here?
> **Is it OK** to eat inside the theater?

To ask if something is allowed, use **Are we allowed to ... ?**

> **Are we allowed to** take pictures?
> **Are we allowed to** ask questions during the lecture?

Useful words
join   to come together with other people
a cell   a phone that you can carry around with you

● Listen for

Here are some important phrases that are connected with going out.

Are you free tomorrow night?
What are you doing tonight?
Would you like to go out?
How about next week?
I'm afraid I'm busy.
I'm busy next week.
I'd love to.

Where would you like to sit?
Smoking or non-smoking?
Can I see your tickets, please?
Would you like to buy a program?

Let me get you a drink.
Did you have a good time tonight?
Thank you for inviting me.
It was a great party.
We really enjoyed the party.

Useful words

free	not doing anything else and so able to do something
busy	already doing something, so that you are not free to do something else
great	very good

Listen to the conversation: Track 9

Friends Katie and Emma are deciding what to do tonight.

A I've got an idea. Let's go to the movies.

B Do you know what's playing?

A Well, there's the new James Daniels movie. We could go and see that.

B I don't really like his movies. They're too long.

A I don't think so, but we don't have to see a movie if you don't want to. What about going bowling?

B I haven't gone bowling in ages! That would be fun.

A Is it OK if I invite Laila?

B Good idea. How about inviting Riku, too? It would be nice to see them both.

A OK. Should I call them?

B Sure. Why not?

A Is there someplace near the bowling alley where we could meet them for a cup of coffee first?

B Yes, there's a café just next to it. Why not meet them there?

A OK, I'll ask them. What time should I say?

B What about five o'clock, inside the café?

A That sounds good. I'll let you know what they say.

 Listen to more phrases and practice saying them: Track 10

Days out

Have a nice day!

If you are visiting a city or a part of a country, these phrases will help you say what you want, ask where things are, and ask for what you need.

Saying what you want to do

To say what you want to do, use **I'd like to ...** .

> **I'd like to** go to the museum.
> **I'd like to** climb the tower.
> **We'd like to** see the art exhibit.

If you are very eager to do something, use **I'd really like to ...** or **I'd love to ...** .

> **I'd really like to** see the Great Wall of China.
> **I'd really like to** take the children to the beach.
> **I'd really like to** take some pictures of the fountain.

> **I'd love to** go to the movies.
> **I'd love to** go hiking in the mountains.
> **I'd love to** visit the palace.

Useful words

a museum	a building where you can look at interesting and valuable objects
a tower	a tall, narrow building, or a tall part of another building
an exhibit	a public display of art or other objects
a beach	an area of sand or stones next to a lake or ocean
a fountain	a structure in a pool or a lake where water is forced up into the air and falls down again
a palace	a large, grand building where a king or queen lives

Talking about your plans

We often say **I'm going to ...** or **I'll** plus the simple form of the verb to talk about what we will do in the future.

> **I'm going to** visit the Palace of Versailles.
> **I'm going to** call to find out if it's open on Sundays.
> **We're going to** take the children with us.

> **I'll** meet you in front of the hotel at 12 o'clock.
> **I'll** go to the Picasso Museum first.
> **We'll** take a train to Washington, DC.

Use **Are you going to ... ?** or **Will you ... ?** to ask someone about their plans.

> **Are you going to** buy a travel guide?
> **Are you going to** visit the Acropolis?
> **Are you going to** take a picnic lunch?

> **Will you** spend all day at the museum?
> **Will you** have time to see the gardens?
> **Will you** take your umbrella with you?

Useful words

find something out	to learn the facts about something
a travel guide	a book for tourists that gives information about a town, an area, or a country
a picnic	a meal that is eaten outdoors
spend	to use your time doing something
umbrella	an object that you hold above your head to protect yourself from the rain

Making suggestions

If two or more people are trying to decide what to do, use **We could ...** or
Shall we ... ?

> **We could** go to the zoo.
> **We could** take a ferry to the island.
> **We could** take him to the science museum.

> **Should we** go to the beach?
> **Should we** go to the club?
> **Should we** try and climb to the top?

To suggest what someone else can do, use **You could ...** .

> **You could** go on a tour of the city.
> **You could** ask Jan to show you around town.
> **You could** take the children to the fair.

Use **How about ... ?** if you have an idea about what to do.

> **How about** taking a boat trip around the harbor?
> **How about** taking a tour of the Capitol Building?
> **How about** going to the National Museum?

> **GOOD TO KNOW!**
> **How about + -ing**
> The verb that comes after **How about** must be in the -ing form.

Useful words

a zoo	a park where animals are kept, and people can go to look at them
a ferry	a boat that regularly takes people or things a short distance across water
an island	a piece of land that is completely surrounded by water
a tour	a trip around an interesting place
a harbor	an area of water next to the land where boats can safely stay

Asking for information

When you are asking for information, you may need to get someone's attention before you can ask a question. To do this, first say **Excuse me**.

> **Excuse me**, is the modern art museum near here?
> **Excuse me**, do you know what time the gardens open?
> **Excuse me**, where can I buy a ticket?

Use **Is ... ?** to ask general questions.

> **Is** the castle interesting?
> **Is** the museum free on Tuesdays?
> **Is** it far to the ice rink?

Use **Is there ... ?** or **Are there any ... ?** to ask whether something exists.

> Excuse me, **is there** a visitor center near here?
> **Is there** a lot to do in Denver?
> **Is there** somewhere to leave our coats?

> **Are there any** cheaper tickets?
> **Are there any** activities for children?
> **Are there any** good hiking trails around here?

To ask about the time, use **What time ... ?**

> **What time** does the park close?
> **What time** is the next guided tour?
> **What time** do I need to be there?

Useful words

a castle	a large building with thick high walls that was built in the past to protect people during wars and battles
an ice rink	a place where people go to skate
a tourist	a person who is visiting a place on vacation
an activity	something that you spend time doing
a guided tour	a trip around an interesting place with someone who tells you about it

To ask about the price of something, use **How much ... ?**

> **How much** is this postcard, please?
> **How much** is a student ticket?
> **How much** are the tickets?

To ask about the time that something will take, use **How long ... ?**

> **How long** does the tour last?
> **How long** is the boat trip?
> **How long** does it take to get there?

To ask how to do something, use **How do you ... ?**

> **How do you** get to the old part of town?
> **How do you** buy tickets?
> **How do you** know which bus to take?

> **GOOD TO KNOW!**
> **How do you + infinitive**
> The verb that comes after **How do you** must be in the simple form.

Asking for things

To ask for something, use **Can I have ... ?** or **Could I have ... ?** To be very polite, use **please** at the beginning or end of the question.

> **Can I have** two tickets, please?
> **Can I have** your travel guide for a minute?
> **Can I have** an audio guide, please?

Useful words	
a postcard	a card with a picture on one side, that you can mail without an envelope
take	to get on a bus, train, or plane in order to travel somewhere
an audio guide	a piece of equipment that gives you spoken information about a place

Could I have two tickets, please?
Could I have a program for tonight's concert?
Could I have three seats together?

Another way of asking for something in a store is **I'd like ...** .

I'd like a map of the area, please.
I'd like two tickets for the 7:30 show.
I'd like seats in the front row if possible.

If it is important for you to have something, you can use **I need ...** .

I need the address of the museum.
She needs two more tickets.
I need a street map of the city.
We need a guide who can speak English.

If you want to ask if something you want is available, use **Do you have ... ?**

Do you have any brochures in English?
Do you have any information on day trips in this area?
Do you have tickets for tomorrow's show?

Useful words

a program	a small book or piece of paper that tells you about a play or concert
a row	a line of seats
an address	the number of the building, the name of the street, and the town or city where a building is
a guide	someone who shows tourists around places such as museums or cities
a brochure	a thin magazine with pictures that gives you information about a place, a product, or a service
a show	a performance in a theater

If you are asking someone if they can do something for you, use **Can you ... ?** or **Could you ... ? Could you ... ?** is slightly more formal than **Can you ... ?** To be very polite, use **please.**

> **Can you** tell me what the hours are?
> **Can you** give me directions to the children's museum?
> **Please can you** show me where we are on this map?

> **Could you** take me to the plaza, please?
> **Could you** check if I've got the right tickets?
> **Could you** tell me the way to the theater?

Asking if something is allowed or permitted

If you need to ask if you can do something, the simplest way is to use **Can I ... ?**

> **Can I** sit here?
> **Can I** take my bag inside?
> **Can we** park here?

If you want to check that someone will not be unhappy or angry if you do something, use **Do you mind if ... ?**

> **Do you mind if** I pay later?
> **Do you mind if** we sit on the grass?
> **Do you mind if** I leave the stroller here?

Useful words

hours	the times that a place opens and closes
a plaza	an open square in a city
check	to make sure that something is correct
park	to stop a vehicle and leave it somewhere
a stroller	a small chair on wheels used for moving a young child around

You can also use **Is it OK ... ?** This is slightly informal, but you can use it in most situations.

> **Is it OK** to take pictures?
> **Is it OK** if we come back later?
> **Is it OK** to bring a friend?

To ask if something is allowed, use **Are we allowed to ... ?**

> **Are we allowed to** take drinks inside?
> **Are we allowed to** come back in again later?
> **Are we allowed to** ask questions?

Saying what you like, dislike, prefer

To talk about things you like, use **I like ...** and to ask someone if they like something, use **Do you like ... ?**

> **I like** visiting modern art galleries.
> **I like** outdoor concerts.
> **I like** this sculpture very much.

> **GOOD TO KNOW!**
> **Like + -ing**
> When **like ...** is followed by a verb, the verb is usually in the -ing form.

> **Do you like** going to concerts?
> **Do you like** modern art?
> **Do you like** looking at castles?

Useful words

outdoor	happening outside and not in a building
a sculpture	a piece of art that is made into a shape from a material like stone or wood

If you like something, but not in a strong way, use **I sort of like ...** .

> **I sort of like** going to movies.
> **I sort of like** the ballet.
> **I sort of like** exploring new places.

If you like something very much, you can say **I really like ...** or **I love ...** .

> **I really like** going walking with friends.
> **I really like** the harbor area.
> **I really like** relaxing in the park.

> **I love** the ruins in Taos.
> **I love** this type of architecture.
> **I love** this museum.

To tell someone what you do not like, use **I don't like ...** .

> **I don't like** bus tours.
> **I don't like** visiting ancient ruins.
> **I don't like** Shakespeare.

To say very strongly that you do not like something, use **I hate ...** .

> **I hate** being late.
> **I hate** horror movies.
> **I hate** traveling by subway.

Useful words

ballet	a type of dancing that needs a lot of skill and in which there are many carefully planned movements
relax	to feel more calm and less worried
architecture	the style of the design of a building
ancient	very old, or from a long time ago
ruins	the parts of a building that remain after something destroys the rest
a horror movie	a very frightening movie that you watch for entertainment
subway	a railway system in a city in which electric trains travel below the ground in tunnels

> **GOOD TO KNOW!**
> **Hate + -ing**
> When **hate** is followed by a verb, the verb is usually in the -ing form.

If you want to say that you like one thing more than another, use **I prefer ...** .
If you want to talk about the thing you like less, use **to**.

> **I prefer** science museums **to** art museums.
> **I prefer** modern art.
> **I prefer** walking **to** biking.

Complaining

You may have to complain about something that you're unhappy with. If you are complaining about something that is happening now, use **It's ...** .

> **It's** too crowded.
> **It's** boring.
> **It's** badly organized.

To talk about an event or an activity that is completed, use **It was ...** .

> **It was** really expensive.
> **It was** a waste of money.
> **It was** difficult to find.

Useful words

crowded	full of people
boring	not interesting
organize	to plan or arrange something
a waste of money	when you spend money on something that is not useful or enjoyable

To talk about something that you are not happy with, use **There's ...** .

> **There's** trash all over the place.
> **There's** nowhere to park.
> **There's** a lot of construction going on.

To talk about something that a place does not have, use **There isn't ...** .

> **There isn't** anywhere to sit.
> **There isn't** any information about the paintings.
> **There isn't** enough room to park.

Useful words

trash   things that people have thrown away because they do not want them

● Listen for

Here are some useful phrases you may hear on your day out.

What language would you like the information in?
Here's a flyer in English.
Do you have a student ID?
The museum's open from nine to three.
The gallery's closed on Sundays.
The next guided tour's at ten.
How many tickets would you like?
They're eight dollars a piece.
You're not allowed to take pictures.
Can I search your bag?
Please leave your things in the coatroom.
Keep off the grass.
Did you enjoy it?

Useful words

a flyer	a piece of paper containing information about a particular subject
search	to look carefully in a place for something or someone
student ID	a card, usually with a picture, that identifies someone is a student
a coatroom	a room in a building where you can leave your coat

Listen to the conversation: Track 11

Scott is visiting his friend Beth, who lives in Boston.

A Do you have any plans for today, Scott?

B I'd like to go to the Boston Common. I really like walking in city parks.

A Really? I prefer being inside. Do you mind if I don't come with you?

B That's fine.

A How about meeting for lunch afterwards?

B Great idea. So, what's the best way to get to the Commons?

A You can take the trolley.

B How long will it take to get there?

A About twenty minutes.

B Is there a visitor center there?

A I think so. OK, have a great morning, and I'll see you later.

Scott is trying to buy tickets to a show for him and Beth.

A Do you have any tickets for the Boston Ballet?

B I've got a few left for this evening.

A What time does the show start?

B At 7.30. So, how many tickets do you want?

A   Two, please. How much are the tickets?

B   105 dollars each.

A   **Are there any cheaper seats?**

B   There are some for 40 dollars if you have a student ID card.

A   **I'm not a student.**

B   Well, there are some in the back for 64 dollars.

A   **OK, I'd like two of those, please.**

 Listen to more phrases and practice saying them: Track 12

Shopping

Can I help you?

The phrases in this section will help you when you go shopping. If you need to buy clothes, food, or things for your house, use these phrases.

Asking for things

To ask for something in a store, use **I'd like ...** or **Could I have ... ?**

> **I'd like** two pounds of potatoes, please.
> **I'd like** a bottle of water.
> **I'd like** two red peppers.

> **Could I have** three oranges, please?
> **Could I have** a book of stamps?
> **Could I have** a shopping bag, please?

You can also say what you are looking for by using **I'm looking for ...** or **I need ...** .

> **I'm looking for** an ereader for my daughter.
> **I'm looking for** a white shirt.
> **I'm looking for** plastic cups.
> **I'm looking for** a present for my mother.

> **I need** a new coat.
> **I need** 8 ounces of mozzarella.
> **I need** batteries for my laptop.

Useful words

a pepper	a hollow green, red, or yellow vegetable with seeds inside
a shopping bag	a plastic or paper bag with handles that you use for carrying shopping
mozzarella	a type of white Italian cheese
an ereader	a small electronic device with a screen that you can read an ebook on
a battery	a device for storing or producing electricity, for example in a radio or a car
a laptop	a small computer that you can carry with you

To ask if a store sells the thing you want, use **Do you sell ... ?** or **Do you have ... ?**

> **Do you sell** light bulbs?
> **Do you sell** balloons?
> **Do you sell** newspapers?

> **Do you have** any mangoes?
> **Do you have** any large suitcases?
> **Do you have** a doll with long hair?

When you decide what you want to buy, use **I'll have ...** or **I'll take ...** .

> **I'll take** these two postcards.
> **I'll take** the blue ones.
> **I'll take** two pineapples.

> **I'll have** strawberry ice cream.
> **I'll have** I'll have the red one.
> **I'll have** half a pound of ham.

Saying what you have to do

If you need to buy something, use **I have to ...** or **I've got to ...** .

> **I have to** buy new shoes.
> **I have to** go to the bakery.
> **I have to** get some bread.
> **We have to** buy some new chairs.

Useful words

a balloon	a round, brightly-colored rubber object that is filled with air or gas
a mango	a large, sweet yellow or red fruit that grows in hot countries
a suitcase	a case for carrying your clothes when you are traveling
a doll	a child's toy that looks like a small person or a baby
a pineapple	a large fruit with sweet yellow flesh and thick, brown skin
a strawberry	a small soft red fruit that has a lot of seeds on its skin
ham	meat from a pig that has been prepared with salt and spices
a bakery	a store where you can buy bread and cakes

I've got to buy a present for Max.
I've got to get a new toothbrush.
I've got to replace my laptop.

You could also use **I need to ...** .

I need to get some apples.
I need to buy a tent.
I need to get a new pair of glasses.

To talk about some shopping that is very important, you use **I really...** .

I really need to find a dress for the party on Saturday.
I really need to find a birthday present for my sister.
I've really got to buy a suit for the interview.

Talking about your plans

To tell someone what you are going to do, use **I'm going to ...** .

I'm going to buy a pair of pants.
I'm going to buy them online.
We're going to buy a bed.

Useful words

a present	something that you give to someone, for example on their birthday
a toothbrush	a small brush that you use for cleaning your teeth
a laptop	a small computer that you can carry with you
a tent	a shelter made of cloth that is held up by poles and ropes, and that you sleep in when you go camping
glasses	two pieces of glass or plastic (= lenses) in a frame, that some people wear in front of their eyes to help them see better
a suit	a jacket and pants or a skirt that are made from the same cloth
an interview	a formal meeting in which someone asks you questions to find out if you are the right person for a job
online	using the Internet or connected to the Internet

To talk about what you're thinking of buying or where you're thinking of going, use **I'm thinking of ...** .

> **I'm thinking of** going to the mall tomorrow.
> **I'm thinking of** going shopping in New York City.
> **I'm thinking of** buying a new car.

For something you would like to do, but that is not certain, use **I hope to ...** .

> **I hope to** find something for under 20 dollars.
> **I hope to** find a cheap sofa.
> **We hope to** find a present for Miyoko.

Expressing opinions

When you look at things in stores, you may want to say what you think of them. Use **I think ...** or **I don't think ...** .

> **I think** this dresser is really beautiful.
> **I think** this shirt will look good on you.
> **I think** the mangoes look good.

> **I don't think** this sweater is warm enough.
> **I don't think** the quality of the material is very good.
> **I don't think** the salespeople are very well trained.

Useful words	
a mall	a large shopping area
cheap	costing little money or less than you expected
a dresser	a piece of furniture in which you keep clothes
suit	to make you look attractive
a sweater	a warm piece of clothing that covers the upper part of your body and your arms
a salesperson	a person who works in a shop
train	to teach someone the skills they need in order to do something

To agree with someone's else's opinion, use **I agree** or **You're right.**

> **I agree** with you that the blue dress is nicer.
> "These shoes are lovely." "**I agree** — I'm going to try some on."
> "This store is much too expensive." "**I agree** — let's go somewhere else."

> "It's too tight around the waist." "**You're right**. I need a bigger size."
> "It's a lot of money to spend on a TV." "**You're right**, but I want a really good one for the World Cup."
> "You don't need another pair of jeans." "**You're right**."

If you are shopping with someone, you may want to ask for that person's opinion about something you are thinking of buying. Use **What do you think ... ?**

> **What do you think** of these pants?
> **What do you think** about getting Jack an MP3 player?
> **What do you think** of this store?

If you are trying to choose between things in a store and you want an opinion from the person you are with, use **Which ... ?**

> **Which** one do you like?
> **Which** dress should I buy?
> **Which** skirt fits best?

Useful words

try something on	to put on a piece of clothing to see if it fits you or if it looks nice
tight	clothes fit closely to your body
waist	the middle part of your body
a skirt	a piece of clothing for women and girls that hangs down from the waist
fit	to be the right size for someone or something
an MP3 player	an electronic device for playing music

Asking for information

For general information, use questions such as **Where ... ?** or **Which ... ?**

> **Where**'s the nearest bank, please?
> **Where** can I find sunglasses?
> **Where** are the dressing rooms?

> **Which** brand do you recommend?
> **Which** batteries do I need to buy for my MP3 player?
> **Which** floor is the children's department on?

If you want to ask if an area of town has a certain store, use **Is there ... ?**

> **Is there** a supermarket near here?
> **Is there** a butcher shop in town?
> **Is there** a parking lot?

You can also use **Is there ... ?** or **Do you have ... ?** to ask if a store has something.

> **Is there** an organic food section?
> **Is there** anyone who can help me carry this to my car?
> **Is there** a dressing room?

Useful words

sunglasses	dark glasses that you wear to protect your eyes from bright light
a dressing room	a room in a clothes shop where you can try clothes
a brand	the name of a product that a particular company makes
recommend	to suggest that someone would find a particular person or thing good or useful
a butcher shop	a store where you can buy meat
a parking lot	an area of ground or a building where people can leave their cars for a period of time
organic	grown without using chemicals

Do you have any other saucepans?
Do you have it in a smaller size?
Do you have any shopping carts?

To ask for information about something you might buy, use **Is this ... ?** or **Is it ... ?**

Is this the only model you have?
Is this the biggest size?
Are these the only colors you have?

Is it made of real leather?
Is it big enough for four people?
Is it free?

To ask for the price of something, use **How much ... ?**

How much is a bottle of orange juice?
How much are the tomatoes, please?
How much is this vase?
How much are the batteries?

To ask whether you can do something, use **Can I ... ?**

Can I pay by credit card?
Can I have it giftwrapped?
Can I have a discount if I buy ten?

Useful words

a saucepan	a deep metal cooking pot, usually with a long handle and a lid
a shopping cart	a large metal basket on wheels that a customer uses
a model	a particular design of a vehicle or a machine
leather	animal skin that is used for making shoes, clothes, bags and furniture
a vase	a container holding flowers
a credit card	a plastic card that you use to buy something and pay for it later
giftwrap	to cover something with paper or cloth so that it can be given as a present
a discount	a reduction in the usual price of something

Saying what you like, dislike, prefer

To say that you like something, use **I like ...** .

> **I like** this store.
> **I like** these shoes a lot.
> **I like** the cakes they sell here.

To say that you like something very much, use **I really like ...** .

> **I really like** the bakery near the university.
> **I really like** this sofa.
> **I really like** looking for bargains.

If you do not like something, use **I don't like ...** .

> **I don't like** these plates very much.
> **I don't like** shopping in big stores.
> **We don't like** standing in line.

> **GOOD TO KNOW!**
> **Like + -ing**
> When **like** is followed by a verb, the verb is usually in the -ing form.

To say that you like one thing more than another, use **I prefer ...** . If you want to talk about the thing you like less, use **to** before it.

> **I prefer** the green one.
> **I prefer** small grocery stores **to** supermarkets.
> **We prefer** fresh vegetables.
> **I prefer** to buy books on the Internet.

Useful words

a sofa	a long, comfortable seat with a back, and usually arms, that two or three people can sit on
a bargain	something that is being sold at a lower price than usual
stand in line	to stand one behind the other in a line of people, waiting for something
fresh	picked, caught, or produced recently
a grocery store	a store that sells food

You can also use **I like ... more than ...** .

> **I like** the yellow one **more than** the red one.
> **I like** the plastic cups **more than** the glass ones.
> **I like** orange juice **more than** apple juice.

Making suggestions

If you are shopping with a friend, use **We could ...** or **Should we ... ?** to make suggestions.

> **We could** look in another store.
> **We could** ask them to order it for us.
> **You could** ask for a discount.

> **Should we** buy the refrigerator today?
> **Should we** get a present for Joe?
> **Should we** go to a bigger store?

If you are eager to do something, you could say **Let's ...** .

> **Let's** buy some flowers.
> **Let's** get the expensive one — it'll be better.
> **Let's** buy new bedding.

Useful words

order	to ask for something to be sent to you from a company
a refrigerator	a large container that is kept cool inside, usually by electricity, so that the food and drink in it stays fresh
bedding	the sheets and pillowcases for a bed

Asking if something is allowed or permitted

To ask someone in a shop if you can do something, use **Can I ... ?**

>**Can I** try on this skirt?
>**Can I** keep the hanger?
>**Can I** return it if I don't like it?
>**Can I** exchange this coat for a different one?
>**Can my daughter** try on this jacket?

A polite way of asking if something is allowed or permitted is **Do you mind if I ... ?**

>**Do you mind if I** open the package?
>**Do you mind if I** try on the earrings?
>**Do you mind if I** taste one of the cherries?

A slightly informal way of asking if something is allowed or permitted is **Is it OK to ... ?**

>**Is it OK** to look inside the box?
>**Is it OK** to try a grape?
>**Is it OK** to take the cellphone out of its box?

Useful words

a hanger	an object for hanging clothes on
a package	a small box, bag or envelope in which an amount of something is sold
a cherry	a small, round fruit with red skin
a grape	a small green or purple fruit, eaten raw or used to make wine

● Listen for

Here are some useful phrases you may hear when out shopping.

Are you being helped?
Can I help you?
What size are you?
Do you need a smaller size?
Would you like me to look for a larger size for you?
What color would you like?
How much were you thinking of spending?
We don't have any in stock just now.
Anything else?
Is it a present for someone?
Do you want me to giftwrap it for you?
Would you like to keep the hanger?
Sorry, cash only.
I'm afraid we don't take credit cards.
Could you sign here, please?
How would you like to pay?
Please enter your PIN.
You can take your card back now.

Useful words

in stock	available for you to buy
cash	money in the form of bills and coins

Listen to the conversation: Track 13

Katie is shopping for clothes with her friend Emma.

A I need to get something to wear to Lola's party on Saturday.

B OK, where do you want to look?

A I really like that dress shop on Main Street, but it's a little expensive.

B Let's go there first and look. We could go somewhere else afterwards if you can't find anything there you can afford.

Katie and Emma are now in the dress shop.

A What do you think of this dress?

B It's nice, but I don't think it's right for a party — it's a little boring.

A You're right. Let's see if there's something better.

B This one would look nice on you.

A I don't like it — it's old-fashioned. I'm looking for something sort of modern. Oh, look — this one's perfect!

B I think so, too. And I really like the color.

A They also have it in blue. Which one do you prefer?

B I like the red one more. But how much is it?

A Wow. It's a lot more than I want to spend.

B Go on, treat yourself! It's the kind of dress you'll wear again and again.

A You're right, Laura. I'll buy it!

 Listen to more phrases and practice saying them: Track 14

Useful words

can afford something	to have enough money to pay for something
boring	dull; not interesting
old-fashioned	no longer used, done or believed by most people
silk	a smooth shiny cloth that is made from very thin threads

Service with a smile

Excellent service!

If you need a service of some sort, or need help or information, these phrases will help you say what you want and ask for what you need.

Greetings

Use **Hello** as a general greeting to people in shops and banks, etc. It is polite to say **Hello** to anyone in any situation.

> **Hello**, ma'am.
> **Hello.** I wonder if you can help me.

Use **Hi** to greet people in more informal situations, for example a salon where you know the hairdresser.

> **Hi**, I'd like to make an appointment with Morgan.
> **Hi**, I've got an appointment with Freya for a haircut at 10:00.

You can use **Good morning, Good afternoon,** or **Good evening** in slightly more formal situations.

> **Good morning**. I'd like some information about travel insurance.

Useful words

a salon	a place where you go to have your hair cut
hair	the fine threads that grow on your head
an appointment	an arrangement to see someone at a particular time
a haircut	an occasion when someone cuts your hair for you
insurance	an agreement that you make with a company in which you pay money to them regularly, and they pay you if something bad happens to you or your property

Use **Goodbye** when you leave a store or bank, etc.

> Thanks for all your help. **Goodbye**.

Goodbye is often shortened to **Bye**. **Bye** is slightly informal.

> Thanks very much. **Bye**.

See you ... is a slightly informal way of saying goodbye, for example to a hairdresser that you know you will see again.

> Thanks very much. **See you** soon!
> Thanks, Louisa. **See you** in a couple of months.

People often say **Have a good day!** or **Have a good weekend!** as you are leaving.

> Goodbye, **have a good day!**
> Bye, **have a good weekend!**

Talking about yourself

Often you will need to tell people information about yourself, such as your name and where you live. To say what your name is, use **My name is ...** .

> **My name is** Emilia Gomez.
> **My name is** Hallie Stern.
> **My husband's name is** Ray Weaver.

Useful words

a couple	two or around two people or things
a month	one of the twelve parts that a year is divided into
a weekend	Saturday and Sunday

To say where you live, use **my address is ...** .

> **My address is** 29 Knoll Road, Austin, TX 78759.
> **My address** in New Zealand **is** 20 John Street, Auckland.
> **My** permanent **address is** 257 West 84 Street, New York, NY, 10024.

To say which country you were born in and lived in as a child, use **I'm from ...** .

> **I'm from** Algeria.
> **I'm from** Buenos Aires, Argentina.
> **We're from** South Korea.

To say where you are from, you can also use **I'm ...** .

> **I'm** Canadian.
> **I'm** Chinese.

You can give other useful information using **I'm ...** .

> **I'm** on vacation.
> **I'm** here for two weeks.
> **I'm** 26.
> **We're** here for three months.

If you want to say that you are living somewhere for a short time, for example because you are on vacation, use **I'm staying ...** .

> **I'm staying** at a hotel.
> **I'm staying** with a host family.
> **We're staying** in a rented house.

Useful words

permanent	continuing forever or for a very long time
be born	to come out of your mother's body and begin life
a host	someone who invites people to stay in their home
rented	used by people who pay money to the owner

Saying what you have to do

To say what service or help you need, you can use **I have to ...** or **I need to ...** .

> **I have to** go to the bank this afternoon.
> **I have to** pick up my jacket from the dry cleaner's.

> **I need to** get my hair cut.
> **I need to** see a dentist.

To say that you need a certain thing, use **I need ...** .

> **I need** some advice.
> **I need** some information about insurance.

To ask what someone has to do, use **Do you have to ... ?**

> **Do you have to** speak to someone at the bank?
> **Do you have to** show your passport?

Useful words

pick up	to go and get someone or something from a place
a dry cleaner's	a store where clothes are cleaned with a special chemical rather than water
a dentist	a person whose job is to examine and treat people's teeth
a passport	an official document that you have to show when you enter or leave a country

Saying what you want to do

To say what you want to do, use **I'd like to ...** .

> **I'd like to** get these clothes washed.
> **I'd like to** transfer some money.
> **I'd like to** see the dentist today.

If you are very eager to do something, use **I'd really like to ...** or **I'd love to ...** .

> **I'd really like to** spend the morning in town.
> **I'd really like to** speak to someone who can help me.
> **I'd really like to** get a hair cut before my vacation.

> **I'd love to** have a cleaning service come every week.
> **I'd love to** have my hair cut at Stefano's but it's so expensive.
> **I'd love to** get some new glasses.

Useful words	
forget	to not remember something
transfer	to make something or someone go from one place to another
eager	wanting to do something very much
advise	to tell someone what you think they should do
a cleaning service	company whose employees clean the rooms and furniture inside a building
expensive	costing a lot of money
glasses	two pieces of glass or plastic in a frame that some people wear in front of their eyes to help them to see

Asking for information

When you are asking for information you may need to get someone's attention before you can ask them a question. To do this, first say **Excuse me**.

> **Excuse me**, where can I get my bag repaired?
> **Excuse me**, is the post office near here?

Use **Is ... ?** to ask general questions about things.

> **Is** the supermarket far from here?
> **Is** it far to the post office?

Use **Is there ... ?** or **Are there any ... ?** to ask whether something exists.

> Excuse me, **is there** a florist near here?
> **Is there** an Internet café in the area?
> **Is there** anyone who can help me?

> **Are there any** shoe stores in this area?
> **Are there any** cafés near here?
> **Are there any** banks nearby?

Useful words

a supermarket	a large shop that sells all kinds of food and other products for the home
a post office	a building where you can buy stamps and send post
a florist	a shop where you can buy flowers
an Internet café	a café where there are computers which allow you to use the Internet
nearby	only a short distance away; close

To ask about the time that something will happen, use **What time ... ?** or **When ... ?**

> **What time** does the store close?
> **What time** do I need to be here?

> **When** is my appointment?
> **When** should I come back?

To ask about the price of something, use **How much ... ?**

> **How much** is an eye exam?
> **How much** are these glasses?
> **How much** would you charge to fix these shoes?

To ask how much time something will take, use **How long ... ?**

> **How long** is the appointment?
> **How long** do I have to wait to see someone?

To ask how to do something, use **How do you ... ?**

> **How do you** open a bank account?
> **How do you** send money to the UK?

Useful words

close	to shut
an eye exam	a test to find out how well you can see
charge	to ask someone to pay money for something
a bank account	an arrangement with a bank where they look after your money for you

Asking for things

To ask for something, use **Can I have ... ?** or **Could I have ... ?** To be very polite, use **please**.

> **Can I have** a receipt, **please**?
> **Can I have** a photocopy of the document, **please**?
> **Can I have** a brochure, **please**?

> **Could I have** a flyer, **please**?
> **Could I have** some information, **please**?
> **Could I have** a list of prices, **please**?

Another way of asking for a service is **I'd like ...** .

> **I'd like** some help, please.
> **I'd like** an appointment for next week, please.
> **I'd like** your opinion.

If it is important for you to have something, you can use **I need ...** .

> **I need** some help.
> **I need** some information.
> **You need** some form of identification.

Useful words	
a receipt	a piece of paper that shows you have received goods or money from someone
a photocopy	a copy of a document that you make using a special machine
a document	an official piece of paper with important information on it
a brochure	a thin magazine with pictures that gives you information about a product or a service
a flyer	a piece of paper containing information about a particular subject
a list	a set of names or other things that are written or printed one below the other
an opinion	what someone thinks about something
a form of identification	a type of a document that proves who you are

To ask if something that you want is available, use **Do you have ... ?**

> **Do you have** a fax machine?
> **Do you have** any flyers on the subject?
> **Do you have** those documents with you?
> **Do you have** your passport?

If you are asking someone if they can do something for you, use **Can you ... ?** or **Could you ... ? Could you ... ?** is slightly more polite and formal than **Can you ... ?** To be polite, use **please** at the beginning or end of these sentences.

> **Can you** give me a receipt, **please**?
> **Can you** call me on my cellphone when it's fixed, **please**?
> **Can you** tell me how much it will cost?
> **Can you** tell me how much money I have in my account?

> **Could you** take a look at my camera?
> **Could you** check that these are the right documents?
> **Could you** fax it to me, **please**?
> **Could you** email the form to me, **please**?

Useful words

a fax machine	a special machine that is joined to a telephone line and that you use to send and receive documents
fix	to repair something
check	to make sure that something is correct
to fax	to send a document to a fax machine
email	to send a written message from one computer to another
a form	a piece of paper with questions on it and spaces where you should write the answers

Making suggestions

If two or more people are trying to decide what to do or buy, use **We could ...** or **Should we ... ?**

> **We could** come back tomorrow.
> **We could** ask them what they charge.
> **We could** show them your passport.

> **Should we** try a different bank?
> **Should we** come back later?
> **Should we** ask for a refund?

To suggest what someone else can do or buy, use **You could ...** .

> **You could** contact your bank in the U.S.
> **You could** get the TV fixed.
> **You could** use the laundromat on Elm Street.

Use **How about ... ?** if you have an idea about what to do or buy.

> **How about** changing the appointment to Friday?
> **How about** asking to speak to the manager?
> **How about** changing your bank?

GOOD TO KNOW!
How about + -ing
The verb that comes after **How about ... ?** must be in the -ing form.

Useful words

a refund	money that is returned to you because you have paid too much, or because you have returned goods to a store
contact	to telephone someone or send them a message or a letter
a laundromat	a place where people pay to use machines to wash and dry their clothes
a manager	a person who controls all or part of a business or organization

Talking about your plans

You will want to talk about things that you will do or buy that day, that week, or that month. For plans that you are sure of, use **I'm going to ...** .

> **I'm going to** see if they can fix it.
> **I'm going to** pay by check.
> **We're going to** cancel the appointment.

To talk about something that you have just decided to do, use **I'll ...** .

> **I'll** ask at the bank.
> **I'll** change the appointment.
> **I'll** try to get a loan.

Use **Are you going to ... ?** or **Will you ... ?** to ask someone about their plans.

> **Are you going to** look around the apartment?
> **Are you going to** ask for a refund?
> **Are you going to** complain?

> **Will you** call the bank?
> **Will you** get the car washed while you're at the garage?
> **Will you** get your money back?

Useful words	
a check	a printed form from a bank that you write on and use to pay for things
cancel	to say that something that has been planned will not happen
a loan	an amount of money that you borrow
an apartment	a set of rooms for living in, usually on one floor and part of a larger building
complain	to say that you are not satisfied with someone or someone

● Listen for

Here are some phrases you are likely to hear and use when asking for or using services.

> Can I help you?
> Can I help you at all?
> It'll be ready tomorrow.
> It's not ready yet.
> We'll call you when it's ready.
> It's ready to be picked up.
> Do you have your receipt?
> Do you need a receipt?
> Do you have some form of I.D.?
> Do you have your passport?
> I'll need to see some form of identification.
> What time is best for you?
> Do you have an appointment?
> How would you like to pay?
> I'll pay the full amount later.

Useful words

ready	prepared and able to be used
pick up	when you go and get something or someone from a place

Listen to the conversation: Track 15

Katie is speaking to her hairdresser.

A Hi, Katie. What can I do for you today?

B Well, I'd like a nice short haircut for the summer.

A Sure. What style?

B I'd really like a haircut that I can wash and let dry naturally.

A OK. Do you have any pictures with you of the style you'd like?

B No, I'm afraid not.

A Well, we could look in a hair magazine and get some ideas. What about this one?

B Oh, I'd love to have my hair cut like that, but it really is *very* short!

A What about this haircut but just a little longer?

B That sounds great.

A How about changing the color of your hair? Have you ever thought about that?

B Oh, how much would it cost?

A Prices start at around 50 dollars.

B No, I don't have that much money with me today. I think I'll just have my hair cut.

A Sure — no problem.

 Listen to more phrases and practice saying them: Track 16

Health

Get well soon!

If you get sick or have an accident, the phrases in this chapter will allow you to talk to a doctor, dentist, or pharmacist. Use them to get the advice or treatment that you need.

Describing the problem

If you need to describe a medical problem, you can use **I have ...** .

> **I have** a temperature.
> **I have** a cold.
> **I have** asthma.

If you want to say which part of your body hurts, use **My ... hurts**.

> **My** back **hurts**.
> **His** foot **hurts**.
> **My** neck **hurts**.

If the pain you have is an ache, you can say which part of your body it is in by using **a/an... ache**.

> **I have** a head**ache**.
> **I have** a stomach**ache**.
> **She has** a tooth**ache**.

Useful words	
temperature	when someone's body is too hot
a cold	an illness that makes liquid flow from your nose
asthma	an illness that makes it difficult to breathe
sore	painful and uncomfortable
your throat	the back of your mouth and inside your neck

You can talk about more general problems using **I feel ...** .

> **I feel** tired all the time.
> **I feel** sick.
> **I feel** like I'm getting a cold

Saying what happened

If you have an accident, you will need to explain what happened. You will need to use a past tense, such as **I fell ...** or **I burned ...** .

> **I had** an accident.
> **I fell** down the stairs.
> **She burned** her hand.
> **I hit** my head.

If your medical problem means that you cannot do something that you should be able to do, you can use **I can't ...** .

> **I can't** sleep.
> **I can't** move my fingers.
> **She can't** bend her arm.

If the accident is serious, and you have broken a bone, use **broke ...** .

> I think **I broke** my arm.
> **He broke** his leg.
> **She broke** a tooth.

Useful words

an accident	when something bad happens to a person by chance
stairs	a set of steps inside a building
burn	to injure a part of your body by fire
bend	to change the position of a part of your body so that it is no longer straight

> **GOOD TO KNOW!**
> In English we say **break my/his/her/your leg**, not break the leg.

Asking for information

When you are asking for information, you may need to get someone's attention before you can ask them a question. To do this, first say **Excuse me**.

> **Excuse me**, is there a hospital nearby?
> **Excuse me**, how do I make an appointment?
> **Excuse me**, where is the X-ray department?

Use **Is there ... ?** to ask whether something exists near to where you are.

> **Is there** a dentist in the area?
> **Is there** a pharmacy on this street?
> **Is there** a doctor here?

When you need to get information about someone or something, start your questions with **What ... ?**, **Which ... ?**, **How ... ?**, **Who ... ?**, or **When ... ?**

> **What**'s this medicine for?
> **What** number do I call for an ambulance?
> **What**'s your doctor's address?
> **What** do I ask the pharmacist for?

Useful words	
break a leg/ arm, etc.	to break a bone or bones in part of your body
an appointment	an arrangement to see someone at a particular time
an X-ray	a picture of the inside of someone's body
a dentist	a person whose job is to examine and treat people's teeth
a pharmacy	store where you can buy medicine
an ambulance	a vehicle for taking people to hospital
a pharmacist	a person whose job is to prepare and sell medicine

Which doctor did you see last time?
Which street is the clinic on?
Which floor is she on?
Which is the best health clinic?

How do I make an appointment?
How often do I take this medicine?
How long will he be in the hospital?
How quickly can I see a doctor?

Who did you see last time?
Who is your doctor?
Who came with you?
Who gave you this medicine?

When will my operation be?
When is the doctor coming?
When do visiting hours start?
When should I take the pills?

Use **What time ... ?** to ask about when things will happen.

What time is your appointment?
What time does the doctor's office open?
What time do I need to be at the hospital?

Useful words

a health clinic — a place where people receive medical advice or treatment
an operation — when a doctor cuts open a patient's body in order to remove, repair or replace a part

Many of the questions you will be asking can be answered by *yes* or *no*. The most common way of starting a question like this is with **Is ... ?**

> **Is** it serious?
> **Is** the hospital far?
> **Is** the health clinic open in the afternoon?

If you want to ask what to do about your problem, use **Should I ... ?**

> **Should I** make another appointment?
> **Should I** stay in bed?
> **Should I** keep taking the pills?

Asking for things

When you want to find out if something is available, use **Do you have ... ?**

> **Do you have** anything for a headache?
> **Do you have** anything for hay fever?
> **Do you have** the doctor's phone number?

If you want to ask for something, start your sentence with **Can I have ... ?**
To be very polite, use **please**.

> **Can I have** an appointment for tomorrow, please?
> **Can I have** a bottle of aspirin, please?
> **Can I please have** a band-aid?

Useful words

a health clinic	a place where people receive medical advice or treatment
a pill	a small solid piece of medicine that you swallow
hay fever	an illness caused by plants that some people get in the summer
an aspirin	a medicine used to reduce pain and fever
a band-aid	a small piece of sticky material that you use to cover small cuts on your body

Can I ... ? is also used in sentences where you are asking if it's OK to do something or if something is possible.

> **Can I** see the dentist this morning?
> **Can I** talk to a nurse?
> **Can I** drive while I'm taking this medicine?
> When **can we** pick up the test results?

If you want to be very polite, you can use **Is it possible to ... ?**

> **Is it possible to** see a different doctor?
> **Is it possible to** get an earlier appointment?
> **Is it possible to** meet the surgeon before my operation?

If you want to buy something in a pharmacy, use **Can I have ... ?** or **I'd like ...** .

> **I'd like** some cough medicine, please.
> **I'd like** a bottle of aspirin.
> **I'd like** some cream for dry skin.

If you are asking someone whether they can do something for you, you should use **Can you ... ?** or **Could you ... ? Could you ... ?** is slightly more polite and formal than **Can you... ?** To be very polite, you can use **please**.

> **Can you** give me something for my earache, please?
> **Can you** send an ambulance right away?
> **Can you** call a doctor, please?
> **Please can you** give me some advice on how to get in shape?

Useful words

a surgeon	a doctor who is specially trained to do operations
cream	a type of medicine that you rub into your skin
earache	pain in your ear
in shape	healthy and strong

Could you take us to the nearest hospital?
Could you check my blood pressure?
Could you put a bandage on this?
Could you lift your arm for me?

Saying what you want to do

A simple and polite way of saying what you want to do is to use **I'd like to ...** .

- I'd like to make an appointment with the doctor.
  I'd like to see a dentist as soon as possible.
  I'd like to talk to the pharmacist.
- I'd like to speak to the doctor.

> **GOOD TO KNOW!**
> It is more polite to say **I'd like to** than simply I want to.

Use **I'd prefer to ...** when you want to do one thing and not another.

I'd prefer to go to a local hospital.
- I'd prefer to see a female doctor.
  I'd prefer to have the operation next week.
  I'd prefer not to take antibiotics.

You can talk about things that are important for you by using **I need ...** .

I need some eyedrops.
He needs an operation on his leg.
You need to see a doctor.
I need to go to the pharmacy.

Useful words

bandage	a long strip of cloth that is wrapped around an injured part of your body
antibiotics	medicine which cures infections by destroying harmful bacteria
local	in or relating to the area where you live
eyedrops	liquid medicine that you put in your eyes

Making suggestions

The most simple way to make a suggestion is to say **We could ...** or **You could ...** .

> **We could** ask the pharmacist.
> **We could** get some tissues at the pharmacy.
> **We could** call his family.

> **You could** try that medicine I gave you.
> **You could** call this number for advice.
> **You could** try and get an appointment for tomorrow.

If you want to suggest doing something with someone else, use **Should we ... ?**

> **Should we** call a doctor?
> **Should we** give him some medicine?
> **Should we** try and eat more fresh fruit and vegetables?

How about ... ? is a slightly informal way of making suggestions.

> **How about** trying vitamins?
> **How about** changing your diet a little?
> **How about** walking to work instead of driving?

> **GOOD TO KNOW!**
> The verb that comes after **How about** must be in the -ing form.

Useful words

a tissue	a piece of thin, soft paper that you use to wipe your nose
your diet	the type of food that you regularly eat
instead of	in the place of someone or something

● Listen for

Here are some useful phrases you are likely to hear or use at the doctor's or the hospital.

How are you?
What can I do for you?
How long have you been feeling like this?
Are you taking any other medicine?
Do you feel sick?
Where does it hurt?
Your test results all look good.
Are you allergic to antibiotics?
I'll give you a prescription.

← My throat is very sore.
I've been feeling sick.
I've got a pain in my side.
I get out of breath very easily.
I'm not sleeping well.
I have no appetite.
I've been getting a lot of headaches.

Glossary

allergic	becoming ill when you eat, touch, or breathe something
a prescription	a piece of paper on which a doctor writes an order for medicine
out of breath	not able to breathe well
your appetite	the feeling that you want to eat

Listen to the conversation: Track 17

Philip isn't feeling well, so he calls his doctor's office to make an appointment.

A Good morning, Dr. Lee's office. How can I help you?

B Good morning. I'd like to make an appointment to see the doctor.

A When would you like to come?

B Is today possible?

A No, today isn't possible, I'm afraid. But I can make an appointment for you with the doctor for tomorrow morning, at... ten o'clock? Is that OK for you?

B Yes, that's fine. Thank you.

A Your name please?

B Philip Walsh.

A We'll see you tomorrow at ten Mr. Walsh.

B Thank you. Goodbye!

A Goodbye.

Philip is at the appointment with the doctor, and they are discussing his symptoms.

A How can I help you?

B My throat is sore, and my head aches.

A Let me have a look. Can you open your mouth, please? Ah yes, the back of your throat is very swollen. How long has it been like this?

B About a week.

A Hmm, that's a long time. You need some antibiotics. Are you allergic to any antibiotics?

B No, I don't think so.

A OK then, I'll give you a prescription. Make sure you take all the pills, even if you start to feel better.

 Listen to more phrases and practice saying them: Track 18

Help!

Don't worry!

If you have a problem and you need help, use these phrases.

Describing the problem

If you are asking somebody for help, you will need to be able to describe the problem. Use **There is ...** to say what the problem is.

> **There's** water all over the floor.
> **There's** a noise coming from the engine.
> **There are** mice in the kitchen.

If the problem is that you do not have something you need, use **There isn't ...** .

> **There isn't** any soap in the bathroom.
> **There isn't** enough food for everyone.
> **There isn't** any gas in the car.
> **There aren't** any towels in my room.

Useful words

an engine	the part of a car that produces the power to make it move
a mouse, *plural* mice	a small animal with a long tail
soap	a substance that you use with water for washing yourself
gas	the fuel which you use in cars and some other vehicles to make the engine go
a towel	a piece of thick soft cloth that you use to dry yourself

For some problems, you can use **I have ...** .

> **I have** a problem.
> **I have** a flat tire.
> **I have** too much work.

If the problem is that you do not have something you need, use **I don't have ...** .

> **I don't have** her address.
> **She doesn't have** enough money.
> **He doesn't have** a car.
> **I don't have** my phone with me.

If the problem is that you are not able to do something, use **I can't ...** .

> **I can't** drive.
> **I can't** turn the heat on.
> **We can't** open the bedroom door.
> **I can't** find my keys.

If you want to say that you do not understand something, use **I don't understand ...** .

> **I don't understand** what he's saying.
> **I don't understand** the instructions.
> **I don't understand** where we have to go.
> **I don't understand** how to use this phone.

Useful words

flat	with not enough air inside
a tire	a thick round piece of rubber that fits around the wheels of cars and bicycles
heat	the equipment that is used for keeping a building warm
turn something on	to make a piece of equipment start working
instructions	things that people tell you to do

Describing people and things

You can describe things that have been lost or stolen using **It's ...** .

> **It's** a black Honda with red seats.
> **It's** gold with three diamonds.
> **It's** a ladies' watch.
> **It's** a green suitcase with wheels.

When you are describing something, you may need to give more facts. Use **It's made of ...** to say what it is made of.

> **It's made of** leather.
> It's a small bag, and **it's made of** velvet.
> The beads are bright blue, and **they're made of** glass.

Useful words

a passport	an official document that you have to show when you enter or leave a country
an accident	when something bad happens to a person by chance, sometimes causing injury or death
glasses	two pieces of glass or plastic in a frame, that some people wear in front of their eyes to help them to see better
a diamond	a hard clear stone that is very expensive and that is used for making jewelery
a suitcase	a case for carrying your clothes when you are traveling
leather	animal skin that is used for making shoes, clothes, and bags
velvet	cloth that is thick and soft on one side
a bead	a small piece of colored glass, wood, or plastic that is used for making jewelery

You may need to describe someone who is lost or who has done something wrong to the police. Use **He's/She's ...** to say how old a person is.

> **He's** five years old.
> **She's** eight.
> **She was** about thirty.
> **He was** about sixty.

Use **He/She has ...** to talk about what someone looks like.

> **She has** short blond hair.
> **He has** a beard.
> **She has** a small mouth.
> **They** both **have** brown eyes.

To talk about someone's clothes, use **He's/She's wearing ...** .

> **She's wearing** jeans and a green T-shirt.
> **She's wearing** an orange blouse.
> **He's wearing** a black jacket.
> **They're wearing** long coats.

Useful words

blond	with pale-colored hair
a beard	the hair that grows on a man's chin and cheeks
a blouse	a shirt for a girl or a woman

Asking for information

You may need someone with a special skill to help you. Use **Is there ...** to ask about where to find that person. You may need to get someone's attention before you can ask them a question. Use **Excuse me** to do this.

> Excuse me, **is there** a garage near here?
> **Is there** a police station near here?
> **Is there** a place in town where I can rent a car?
> **Is there** anyone who fixes bikes here?

You may want to find out how to do something to help with your problem. Use **How ... ?**

> **How** do I find his phone number?
> **How** can we find a plumber?
> **How** do I turn the computer on?
> **How** can she get help with her car?

If you want to know where to go to get help with your problem, use **Where ... ?**

> **Where** is the nearest police station?
> **Where** is the lost and found?
> **Where** can he get his phone fixed?
> **Where** can I buy a new battery?

Useful words

a garage	a place where you can have your car repaired
a police station	the local office of the police
rent	to pay the owner of something in order to use it yourself
fix	to repair something
a plumber	a person whose job is to put in and repair water and gas pipes
lost and found	a place where things that people have lost are stored
a battery	a small object that provides electricity for things such as radios

Asking for things

If you want to ask for something that will help with your problem, use **Can I have ... ?**

> **Can I have** the phone number of an electrician?
> **Can I have** another form, please?
> **Can I have** another blanket, please?

If you want to find out if something is available, use **Do you have ... ?**

> **Do you have** a fax machine?
> Excuse me, **do you have** a lost and found?
> Excuse me, **do you have** this document in English?

If you are asking someone whether they can do something for you, you should use **Can you ... ?** or **Could you ... ? Could you ... ?** is slightly more polite and formal than **Can you ... ?** To be very polite, you can use **please**.

> **Can you** help me, please?
> **Can you** call the police?
> **Can you** please fix my bike?

> **Could you** recommend an electrician?
> **Could you** please show me how the shower works?
> **Could you** fix my laptop?

Useful words

an electrician	a person whose job is to repair electrical equipment
a form	a piece of paper with questions on it and spaces where you should write the answers
a document	an official piece of paper with important information on it
recommend	to suggest that someone would find a particular person or thing good or useful
a shower	a thing that you stand under, that covers you with water so you can wash yourself
a laptop	a small computer that you can carry with you

Saying what you want to do

To say what you want to do about your problem, use **I'd like to ...** .

> **I'd like to** make a complaint.
> **I'd like to** make a call.
> **I'd like to** speak to a police officer.

If you know that you do not want to do something, use **I don't want to ...** .

> **I don't want to** stay in this room.
> **I don't want to** leave my car here.
> **We don't want to** go to the hotel without our luggage.

Saying what you have to do

If it is important for you to do something, use **I have to ...** or **I need to ...** .

> **I have to** go to the American embassy.
> **I have to** leave my room by eleven o'clock.
> **I have to** tell my wife that we're safe.

> **I need to** speak to my lawyer.
> **I need to** make a call.
> **I need to** call an electrician.

Useful words

a complaint	when you say that you are not satisfied
a call	a telephone conversation
a police officer	a member of the police force
an embassy	the building where people who represent a foreign country work
a lawyer	a person whose job is to advise people about the law

Making suggestions

If two or more people are trying to decide what to do about a problem,
use **We could ...** or **Should we ... ?**

> **We could** go by train instead.
> **We could** ask my sister to help us.
> **We could** borrow some money.

> **Should we** call the police?
> **Should we** leave the car here?
> **Should we** try and fix it ourselves?

To suggest what someone else can do about a problem, use **You could ...** .

> **You could** try switching it off and on again.
> **You could** try a new battery.
> **You could** ask for advice at the reception desk.

Use **How about ... ?** if you have an idea about what to do about a problem.

> **How about** asking Mahmoud for help?
> **How about** taking it to the garage?
> **How about** calling that electrician Marco knows?

Useful words

borrow	to use something that belongs to another person for a period of time and then return it
fix	to repair something
switch something off	to stop electrical equipment from working by operating a small control
switch something on	to make electrical equipment start working by operating a small control
reception	the desk in a hotel or large building that you go to when you first arrive

> **GOOD TO KNOW!**
> **How about + -ing**
> The verb that comes after **How about** must be in the -ing form.

Talking about your plans

We often say **I'm going to ...** to talk about what we will do in the future.
Use **Are you going to ... ?** to ask someone about their plans.

> **I'm going to** call the garage.
> **I'm going to** tell the police.
> **I'm going to** call for help.
> **We're going to** call an electrician.

> **Are you going to** fix the car today?
> **Are you going to** take it back?
> **Are you going to** complain?

Use **Will you ... ?** to ask if someone is going to do something.

> **Will you** call us when it's ready?
> **Will you** fix the light at the same time?
> **Will you** charge us extra for this?

Useful words

complain	to say that you are not satisfied with someone or something
charge	to ask someone to pay money for something
extra	more than the normal amount

● Listen for

Here are some key phrases you are likely to hear when you have some kind of problem.

What's the problem?
What happened?
Is there anything I can do to help?
Can I have your insurance information?
What was taken?
Can I have your address, please?
Can I have your driver's licence?
Were there any witnesses?
Please fill out this form.

Can you help me?
I need some help.
I have a problem that I need help with.
There's been an accident.
My car broke down.
The shower/phone/TV doesn't work.
Could you fix my watch/shoes/bag?
Could you change the tire/oil?

Useful words

insurance	an agreement that you make with a company in which you pay money to them regularly, and they pay you if something bad happens to you or your property
information	the facts about something
a driver's licence	a card that shows that you have passed a driving test, and that you are allowed to drive
a witness	a person who saw an event such as an accident or a crime
break down	to stop working

Listen to the conversation: Track 19

Katie's bag has been stolen. She's calling her father for help.

A Hi Dad. I've got a problem. I'm in a café, and someone's stolen my bag. I don't know what to do.

B Have you called the police?

A No, I wasn't sure if I should.

B You could ask the café owners to call them.

A OK, I'll do that. It's terrible, Dad. I've lost my money, my keys – everything! And I'm worried the people in the café won't believe me. Could you come over and help me?

B I'm really sorry, but I have to be in a meeting in ten minutes. How about calling Mom?

A OK, I'll call her. Thanks, Dad.

Scott missed his train, and he needs to get to an important meeting. He is talking to his colleague Laura.

A Hi, Laura, I need some help.

B Sure, what's the problem?

A I missed my train, and I need to be in Chicago by 5 o'clock this afternoon.

B How about flying?

A Could you check the times for me? I'm not on the Internet here.

B Are you coming back tomorrow?

A No, I'm going to meet Andrea on Thursday.

B OK, there's a flight at 12 o'clock. You need to get to the airport an hour before.

A How do I get to the airport from here?

B It's probably best to take a taxi.

A OK, thanks for your help, Laura.

 Listen to more phrases and practice saying them: Track 20

Calling and writing

Getting in touch

The phrases in this unit will help you communicate with people by phone, letter, email, and text.

Making a phone call

If you want to tell someone that you need to make a phone call, use **I need to ...** .

> **I need to** make a call
> **I need to** call my wife.
> **I need to** call my brother.

To ask for a phone number, use **Do you have ... ?**

> **Do you have** Mrs. Kay's number, please?
> **Do you have** the number of a taxi company?
> **Do you have** his cell number?

You can also ask questions using **What ... ?**

> **What's** her phone number?
> **What's** the code for the United States?
> **What** number do I dial for room service?

Useful words

a cell	a phone that you can carry around with you
a code	a group of numbers or letters that come at the beginning of a phone number
dial	to press the buttons on a telephone in order to call someone
room service	when meals are brought to your room in a hotel

When the person you're calling answers

Once you've made the call and someone answers, you will need to tell them who you are. Use **Hello, it's ...** .

> **Hello**, **it's** Marta Fuentes.
> **Hello** Mr. Hall, **it's** Alex Ronaldson.
> **Hello**, is Stephanie in? **It's** Marie.

To explain more about who you are, use **I'm ...** .

> **I'm** a colleague of Amalia's.
> **I'm** a friend of Mei's.
> **I'm** Mr. Lin's daughter.

To check that you are speaking to the right person, use **Is this ... ?**

> **Is this** Jorge?
> **Is this** Dr. Gardner?
> **Is this** the police station?

If you want to ask for somebody, use **Is ... there?** or **Can I speak to ... ?**

> **Is** Oliver **there**?
> **Is** your dad **there**?
> **Is** Mrs. Gomez **there**?

> **Can I** please **speak to** Rebecca?
> **Can I speak to** one of your parents?
> **Can I speak to** someone in the sales department?

Useful words

a colleague	a person someone works with
a department	one of the sections in an organization

GOOD TO KNOW!
If the person you want to speak to is not there, you may be told
Sorry, he's not here or **Sorry, she's not in.**
If the person is there, you be asked **Who's calling, please?**
Answer by saying your name.

We often start a phone conversation, especially with someone we know,
by asking about their health, using **How are you?**

> Hello, Kendra. **How are you?**
> Hi, it's Chuck. **How are you?**

GOOD TO KNOW!
To answer that question, use **I'm fine, thanks** or **I'm good, thanks.**
If you are not well, you could say **Not great, really** or **Not too good,
actually.**

Saying why you're calling

To say why you are calling, use **I'm calling about ...** or **I'm calling to ...** .

> **I'm calling about** tomorrow night.
> **I'm calling about** your ad in the paper.
> **I'm calling about** the job.

> **I'm calling to** talk to Marie.
> **I'm calling to** find out whether you can repair our water heater.
> **I'm calling to** get some information about vacations in Spain.

Useful words

an ad	information that tells you about something such as a product, an event, or a job
repair	to fix something that has been damaged or is not working properly
a water heater	a piece of equipment that provides hot water for a house

To explain where you are or what company or organization you are from, use **I'm calling from ...** .

> **I'm calling from** work.
> **I'm calling from** the doctor's office.
> **I'm calling from** Mr. Brigham's office.

If you want to ask whether you can do something, use **Can I ... ?**

> **Can I** leave a message?
> **Can I** call back later?
> **Can I** give you my cellphone number?

To ask someone else to do something, use **Could you ... ?**

> **Could you** ask her to call me, please?
> **Could you** put me through to Johanna, please?
> **Could you** give her a message?

Giving information

When you make a phone call, you may be asked to give your own phone number. Use **My number is ...** .

> **My** home **number is ...**
> ... and **my** cell **number is ...**
> **The** hotel **phone number** is ...

Useful words

a message	a piece of information that you send to someone
call (someone) back	to call someone in return for a call they made to you
put someone through	to connect someone to someone else on the phone

To give details of where you can be contacted, use **You can contact me on ...** or **You can contact me at ...**.

> **You can contact me at** (617) 555-3264.
> **You can contact me on** my cell.
> **You can contact me at** my sister's number.

Answering the phone

You usually say **Hello** when answering the phone. At work, people sometimes answer by saying their name.

If the person who is calling asks for you, say **Speaking** or **This is ....**

> "Can I speak to Lily, please?" "**This is Lily.**"
> "Is Mrs. Roberts there, please?" "Yes, **speaking.**"

To ask what the person calling wants to do, use **Would you like ... ?**

> **Would you like** to leave a message?
> **Would you like** him to call you back?
> **Would you like** to call back later?

Ending a phone call

When you end a phone call, say **Goodbye** the same way you would if you were leaving someone. This is often shortened to **Bye.**

> Thanks for your help. **Goodbye**.
> OK, then. **Goodbye**.

> **Bye,** Raymond! Talk to you later!
> **Bye.** See you soon.

When you say goodbye, you may want to say hello to someone else. In an informal situation, use **Say hello to ...** , and in a very formal situation, use **Give ... my best wishes.**

> **Say hello to** your family.
> **Say hello to** your sister for me.

> **Give** your father **my best wishes**.
> **Give** Ning **my best wishes**.

● **Listen for**

Here are some useful phrases you may hear when using the telephone.

Who's calling, please?
Please hold.
Hold on a minute. I'll get him.
You've got the wrong number.
Do you have the extension?
His line is busy.
I'll put you through.
Please leave a message after the tone.
Please call back later.
Thanks for calling.

Useful words	
hold	to wait on the phone
extension	the number of a telephone that is connected to a main telephone in an organization
busy	already being used
put someone through	to connect you to someone else on the telephone

Writing letters and emails

Here are some useful phrases for writing letters and emails.

Dear Paul,
Hi Marta!

Love, Naima
Lots of love, Charlotte

All the best, Sahar

Regards, Minh
Best regards, Bella
Yours, Sujata

To: nadia@ntlworld.com

Cc:

Subject: Tomorrow evening

Hi Clara!
Do you want to go to the movies tomorrow evening? Penelope Cruz's new movie is on at 8.30.

If not, how about lunch on Saturday?

See you soon, I hope.

Love,
Nadia

GOOD TO KNOW!
When you say your email address, say **at** for @ and **dot** for .
So Nadia's email address is nadia at ntlworld dot com.

157 North Street — Your address
Newtown
MA 02458

February 15, 2012 — The date

Dear Isabella,

Thanks very much for your last letter. It was great to hear all your news. You seem to be having a great time in China!

Thanks also for the pictures. China looks amazing, and it was good to see you looking so well and so happy.

There's not much happening here. I'm studying hard. I need to get good grades to get into a good journalism program next year. I should do well in English and history, but I'm worried about math — it's so hard!

Your mother said you may be coming home for a week or two in August. If you are, let me know the dates, and we can arrange to meet up.

Hope to see you then!

Martina

Mr. Andrew Kennedy
37 River Road
Los Angeles, CA 90013 ——————— The zip code
comes after
the state.

Starting a formal letter or email

Dear Mr. Chen,
Dear Madam,
Dear Sir or Madam,

Ending a formal letter or email

Yours truly, Anton Smith
Sincerely yours, Allie Sharpe

Ending a formal letter or email in a slightly more friendly way

Best wishes, Tanisha Brown
Regards, Tony Bishop

1500 35th Avenue
Apartment 2A
Phoenix, AZ 85032

Your address

The Manager
Munchies Restaurant
39 Bridgetown Road
TeÜe, AZ 85281

Name and address of the person/company you are writing to

June 2, 2012

The date

Dear Sir/Madam,

I am writing to coÜlain about a meal we had in your restaurant last Wednesday.

I had reserved a table for four for my wife's birthday, but when we arrived there were no free tables, and we had to wait more than half an hour to get one.

My wife's steak was burned, and the waiter was very rude when we told him. From a menu of eight desserts, only two were available, and they were terrible.

I feel that we were treated very badly, and would like a refund for at least half the bill.

Sincerely,

Travis Wilson

Travis Wilson

Texting

Texting is a very popular and quick way to communicate. We often use special abbreviations for texting. Here are some common ones.

@	at	cul	see you later	syl	see you later
2	to *or* two	gr8	great	thx	thanks
2day	today	ic	I see	u	you
2moro	tomorrow	l8	late	w8	wait
4	for	l8r	later	wan2	want to
aml	all my love	lo	hello	wk	week
b4	before	m8	mate	wrk	work
btw	by the way	pls	please	xlnt	excellent
c	see	r	are	y	why
cm	call me	some1	someone		
cu	see you	sry	sorry		

Listen to the conversation: Track 21

Katie is trying to call her friend Saskia. Saskia's father answers the phone.

A Hello.

B Oh, hello Mr. Greene. It's Katie. Can I speak to Saskia, please?

A She's not here at the moment.

B Hmm. I'm calling about the play we're going to tomorrow night.

A Would you like to leave a message?

B That's a good idea. Could you ask her to meet me at the theater at 7 o'clock? If she can't, she should leave a message on my cell or text me.

A Fine, Katie. I'll tell her.

B Thanks, Mr. Greene.

A No problem. It was nice to talk to you.

Rudi has seen an ad for a job he is interested in. He calls the number.

A Hello. Could I speak to Mr. Jenkins, please?

B Speaking.

A My name's Rudi Thorne, and I'm calling about the job in your café.

B Have you worked in a café before?

A Yes, my uncle has a café in Brooklyn and I worked for him in the summer.

B That's good. Would you be able to come in for an interview?

A   OK. What would be a good time?

B   I'm not sure yet because my colleague Doug Young wants to be at the interviews. Can I call you back later?

A   Of course. I'll give you my number.

 Listen to more phrases and practice saying them: Track 22

Work

At work

Most types of work involve a lot of speaking. You have to arrange to meet people, and you have to speak to people who are buying things from you. The phrases in this unit will help you in all these different work situations.

Greetings

Use **Hello** as a general greeting. It is polite to say **Hello** to anyone in any work situation.

> **Hello**, Anton.
> **Hello**, Dr. Lewis.

Use **Good morning, Good afternoon,** or **Good evening** in more formal work situations, for example if you are giving a talk to a large group of people.

> **Good morning**, Carina.
> **Good afternoon**, everyone. I'd like to start by thanking you all for coming here.

Often, when you are at work, you meet people you do not know. You need to know how to greet these people. To tell someone your name, use **Hello, I'm ...**

> **Hello**, **I'm** Carlos Sanchez.
> **Hello**, **I'm** Lanying Peng.

If a person tells you their name, reply by saying **Pleased to meet you** or **Nice to meet you**. Then tell them your name by first saying **I'm ...** .

> **Pleased to meet you**. I'm Carole Durand.
> **Nice to meet you**. I'm Patricia Chapman.

You may also want to tell the person what your job is in the company. To do this, say **I'm ...** .

>> **I'm** the marketing manager for Latin America.
>> **I'm** the head of sales for Western Europe.

Use **Goodbye ...** when you leave someone at work.

>> **Goodbye**, Frida.

See you ... is a slightly informal way of saying goodbye to someone you know you will see again.

>> **See you** later.
>> **See you** tomorrow.
>> **See you** on Thursday.

Introducing people

You may want to introduce a new person to a colleague. To do this, use **this is ...** saying their full name after.

>> Leila, **this is** Chen Wang.
>> Marco, **this is** Yuko Miyuki.
>> Keisha , **this is** Anna-Maria Delgado. Anna-Maria, **this is** Keisha Walker.

Useful words

marketing	the work of advertising and selling a product
a manager	a person who controls all or part of a business or organization
a head	the person who is in charge of a business or organization
sales	the part of a company that sells its products or services
later	at a time in the future
tomorrow	the day after today
introduce	to tell people each other's names so that they can get to know each other
a colleague	a person that someone works with

Talking about your plans

When you are with your colleagues, you may want to talk about things that you will do that day, that week, or that month. For plans that you are sure of, use **I'm going to ...** .

> **I'm going to** email Faisal this morning.
> **I'm going to** call the Beijing office today.
> **We're going to** meet Channa to talk about book sales.

To talk about your plans, you can also use **I plan to ...** .

> **I plan to** finish the job next month.
> **I plan to** visit the Seoul office in June.
> **I plan to** travel later this year.

You can also use **I intend to ...** .

> **I intend to** ask him that question when we meet.
> **I intend to** work on the report this Friday.
> **I intend to** invite her to the meeting.

To talk about a plan that you are not totally sure about, you can use **I hope to ...** .

> **I hope to** write the report this week.
> **I hope to** meet with Francine while I'm in Ontario.
> **We hope to** finish the project by December 12th.
> **They hope to** come to the meeting in June.

Useful words

email	to send a written message from one computer to another
an office	a place where people work sitting at a desk, or the people in that place
sales	the number of things that a company sells
a report	a piece of writing that gives information about a subject
invite	to ask someone to come to an event
a meeting	an event at which a group of people come together to discuss things or make decisions
a project	a plan that takes a lot of time and effort

Use **Are you going to ... ?** or **Will you ... ?** to ask someone about their plans.

> **Are you going to** ask Guy to come to the meeting?
> **Are you going to** email the sales team, too?
> **Are you going to** meet Per while you're in Stockholm?
> **Is he going to** tell you when he has finished?

> **Will you** finish on time?
> **Will you** be at the meeting tomorrow?
> **Will you** ask Roberta to comment on the report?
> **Will he** give us the information?

Making suggestions

To say to a colleague that you will do something, use **I can ...** .

> **I can** invite Yuko to the meeting.
> **I can** check these figures.
> **I can** speak to Mi Yon, if you like.

You can also use **I'll ...** to offer to do something.

> **I'll** write the introduction.
> **I'll** order another computer.
> **I'll** email Santiago, if you like.

> **GOOD TO KNOW!**
> When people use **I can ...** or **I'll ...** to say they will do something,
> they sometimes add **if you like** at the end of the sentence.

Useful words

a team	any group of people who work together
comment	to give your opinion or say something about something
check	to make sure that something is correct
figures	amounts or prices expressed as numbers
an introduction	the part at the beginning of a piece of writing that tells you what the piece of writing is about
order	to ask for something to be sent to you from a company

To suggest something that you and your colleagues could do, use **We could ...** .

> **We could** give the work to someone else.
> **We could** ask Diana for advice.
> **We could** refuse to pay them.

Another way to suggest something that you and your colleagues could do is **Should we ... ?**

> **Should we** finish now?
> **Should we** change the date of the meeting?
> **Should we** discuss this with Tino?

Saying what you have to do

To tell your colleagues that it is very important that you do something, use **I have to ...** .

> **I have to** finish this before I leave.
> **I have to** email Cyrus and tell him.
> **You have to** call the customer when it's ready.

Another way to say what you have to do is to use **I need to ...** .

> **I need to** call Bill this morning.
> **I need to** finish this report today.
> **You need to** write down the customer's phone number.

Useful words

advice	what you say to someone when you are telling them what you think they should do
refuse	to say that you will not do something
a date	a particular day and month or a particular year
discuss	to talk about something
a customer	someone who buys something from a shop or website

When you want to say that you should do something, use **I should ...** .

> **I should** email Henrik, too.
> **I should** offer the job to Sam.
> **I should** let them know I don't want the job so they can offer it to someone else.

To ask what someone has to do, use **Do you have to ... ?**

> **Do you have to** tell your boss?
> **Do you have to** give them an answer now?
> **Do you have to** be in the office tomorrow?

Asking for information

The simplest way of asking if something is a particular thing is **Is it ... ?**

> **Is it** quick?
> **Is it** easy to use?
> **Is it** expensive?

To ask whether there is something, use **Is there ... ?**

> **Is there** a printer?
> **Is there** a coffee machine here?
> **Are there** any extra chairs we could use?

Useful words

a job	the work that someone does to earn money
offer	to ask someone if they would like to have something
a boss	the person in charge of you at the place where you work
expensive	costing a lot of money
a printer	a machine for printing copies of computer documents on paper

To ask for information about something, use **What ... ?**

> **What**'s her name?
> **What**'s his email address?
> **What** do you think?

To ask about the place that something or someone is, use **Where ... ?**

> **Where** is Eduardo?
> **Where** is the fax machine?
> **Where** did Ali go?

To ask about the time that something will happen, use **When ... ?**

> **When** can we meet?
> **When** does she start work?
> **When** does Mira usually leave the office?

Asking for things

To ask a colleague if you can have something, use **Can I ... ?**

> **Can I** use your phone, please?
> **Can I** have her phone number?
> **Can I** see those figures, please?

A slightly more polite way to ask a colleague if you can have something is **Could I ... ?**

> **Could I** borrow this book, please?
> **Could I** use your computer?
> **Could I** sit here for a moment, please?

Useful words

a fax machine	a machine that is joined to a telephone line, and that allows you to send and receive documents
borrow	to use something that belongs to someone else for a period of time and then return it

To ask a colleague if they can do something for you, use **Can you ... ?**

> **Can you** help me with the printer, please?
> **Can you** pass me those papers, please?
> **Can you** check these figures, please?

A slightly more polite way to ask a colleague if they can do something for you is **Could you ... ?**

> **Could you** send me that report, please?
> **Could you** speak to Jingfei about the problem?
> Please **could you** close that door?

GOOD TO KNOW!
When people are asking for something using **Can I/Could I ... ?** or **Can you/Could you ... ?** they often add **please** to be polite.

Apologizing

Sometimes at work, there are problems and we make mistakes. When this happens, we may need to say we are sorry to a colleague or a customer.
To apologize, use **I'm sorry ...** or **Sorry ...** .

> **I'm sorry**. I've forgotten your name.
> **I'm sorry**. I forgot to bring those figures with me.
> **I'm sorry** I'm late.

> **Sorry** I have to leave now.
> **Sorry**. I didn't hear what you were saying.
> **Sorry**. I didn't introduce you.

Useful words

pass	to give an object to someone
apologize	to say that you are sorry
forget	to not remember something
late	after the time that something should start or happen

If you have to tell a colleague or a customer that there is a problem or that something bad has happened, start your sentence with **I'm afraid ...** .

> **I'm afraid** I'm going to be late.
> **I'm afraid** I can't come to the meeting.
> **I'm afraid** there's a problem with your order.
> **I'm afraid** the meeting has been canceled.

GOOD TO KNOW!

If someone apologizes to you, reply **That's all right** or **No problem.** This lets the person who is apologizing know that you are not angry or that the problem is not important.

Expressing opinions

If you want to give your opinion about something, use **I think ...** .

> **I think** these meetings are very useful.
> **I think** we should start now.
> **I think** you're right.

You can also give your opinion of something by saying **In my opinion ...** .

> **In my opinion**, it is too expensive.
> **In my opinion**, we should give the job to Mari Sato.
> **In my opinion**, she's the wrong person for the job.

Useful words

an order	the thing that someone has asked for
cancel	to say that something that has been planned will not happen
an opinion	what someone thinks about something
useful	helpful for doing something
right	correct

To ask someone for their opinion, say **What do you think of ... ?**

> **What do you think of** their products?
> **What do you think of** Kim's report?
> **What do you think of** these meetings?

You can also ask someone for their opinion by saying **What's your opinion of ... ?**

> **What's your opinion of** the new manager?
> **What's your opinion of** Jonas?

Agreeing and disagreeing

If you think that what someone has said is right, say **I agree ...** .

> **I agree**. I think it's very successful.
> **I agree** with Steve.
> Yes, **I agree** with you.

You can also agree with what someone has said by saying **You're right**.

> **You're right**. Sales have to increase.
> **You're right**. We've improved a lot over the years.
> I think **you're right**. She's a very good manager.

Useful words
a product	something that you make or grow in order to sell
successful	doing or getting what you wanted
increase	to get bigger in some way
improve	to get better

If you think that what someone has said is wrong, say I **disagree ...** .

> I **disagree**. I think she's very good at her job.
> I **disagree** with you here.
> I'm afraid I **disagree**.

GOOD TO KNOW!
When people say I **disagree**, they often start the sentence with
I'm afraid. This sounds more polite.

● Listen for

Here are some important phrases you are likely to hear and use at work.

Can I speak to Taylor Jackson, please?
Can I say who is calling, please?
I'm afraid she's not at her desk.
Can I take a message?
Will you be at the meeting?
Is everyone here?
Have you met Charles?
Thanks for all your work on this.
Thanks for finishing this so quickly.
I don't think these figures are accurate.
I've checked the figures.
The report contains some mistakes.
Have you read the report?
I need to check my email.
I got an email from him this morning.
She sent me an email yesterday.
I'll need to speak to my manager.

Useful words

a desk	a table that you sit at to write or work
a message	a piece of information that you send to someone
accurate	correct
a mistake	something that is not correct

Listen to the conversation: Track 23

Two people who work for the same company meet for the first time at a sales conference.

A   Hello, I'm Yasmin Peters.

B   Pleased to meet you. I'm Jim Harker.

A   Do you work in sales, too?

B   Yes, I'm the sales manager for Eastern Europe.

A   Could I sit here for a moment? I've been standing all day!

B   Of course — take a seat. What did you think of the talk today?

A   I thought it was really good.

B   I agree. Jenny Hayes is a really good speaker.

A   You're right — she's excellent.

B   I'm afraid I have to go now. I need to catch a train to the airport, and I don't know how often the trains run.

A   That's all right. I can look up train times on my cellphone, if you like.

B   Could you? That would be great.

A   What time is your flight?

B   Eight o'clock, but I have to be at the airport an hour before.

A   Well, there's a train in fifteen minutes.

B   That sounds perfect. It was nice meeting you, Yasmin.

A   You too, Jim. See you again at the winter sales conference!

 Listen to more phrases and practice saying them: Track 24

studying

In the classroom

If you are in school or college, the phrases in this section will help you to talk about your studies. You will be able to use them in class, to find information you need, and to express your opinions about the subjects you are studying.

Asking for information

When you need to get information about something, start your questions with **What ... ?, Which ... ?, Who ... ?, Where ... ?,** or **When ... ?**

What's this book about?
What does the word fluent mean?

Which room is the math class in?
Which computer should I use?

Who do you have for chemistry?
Who should I give the money to?

Where are the new textbooks?
Where is my bookbag?

When is lunch?
When is your next class?

Useful words

fluent	able to speak a particular language easily and correctly
chemistry	the science of the structure of gases, liquids, and solids, and how they change
a textbook	a book containing facts about a particular subject that is used by students

A common way of asking how to do something is to use the phrase
How do you ... ?

>**How do you** spell that?
>**How do you** divide a small number by a bigger number?
>**How do you** turn this computer on?

Use **Is there ... ?** or **Are there any ... ?** to ask whether something exists.
You use these phrases especially when you want to have something to use.

>**Is there** any paper left?
>**Is there** an extra laptop in here?
>**Are there** any pens in that box?
>**Are there** any more calculators?

If you want to ask your teacher for advice, use **Should I ... ?**

>**Should I** write on both sides of the paper?
>**Should I** put labels on the diagram?
>**Should I** rewrite it?

Useful words

divide	to find out how many times one number can fit into another number
extra	not being used by anyone else
a laptop	a small computer that you can carry with you
a calculator	a small electronic machine that you use to calculate numbers
a label	a word or phrase written on something to show what it is
a diagram	a simple drawing used to explain something
rewrite	to write something in a different way in order to improve it

Expressing opinions

You may be asked to express an opinion about what you are studying.
Use **I think ...** .

> **I think** the answer is 354.
> **I think** "Tom Sawyer" is a great book.
> **I think** the poet is writing about his childhood.
> **I think** we should try the experiment again.

To say that you do not think something is true, use **I don't think ...** .

> **I don't think** this translation is very good.
> **I don't think** the information on this website is very reliable.
> **I don't think** the author would agree.
> **I don't think** the library has that book.

To ask for someone's opinion about the quality of something, use **What do you think of ... ?**

> **What do you think of** Mr. Cowell's class?
> **What do you think of** the science lab here?
> **What do you think of** the sports facilities?

Useful words	
a poet	a person who writes poems (= pieces of writing in which the words are chosen for their beauty and sound, and arranged in short lines)
childhood	the period of time when you are a child
an experiment	a scientific test that you do in order to discover what happens to something
a translation	a piece of writing or speech that has been put into a different language
reliable	probably correct
a library	a place where books, newspapers, DVDs, and music are kept for people to use and borrow
a lab	a building or a room where scientific work is done
facilities	something such as rooms, buildings, or pieces of equipment that are used for a particular purpose

To agree with someone's opinion, use **I agree** or **You're right.** If you want to say who you agree with, use **with**.

> "Miss Grandison is a great teacher." "**I agree**. I love her class."
> **I agree** that Gandhi was a great man.
> **I agree with** Amy — it's good to take a break from studying now and then.

> "I think this chemical must be sulphur." "**You're right**."
> I think **you're right**.
> **Dana is right**. The French Revolution began in 1789.

If you do not agree with someone, you can use **I don't think so.**

> "It's good to listen to music while you study." "**I don't think so**."
> "This homework is easy." "**I don't think so**. Can you help me with it?"
> "Economics is really interesting." "**I don't think so**. I think it's really boring."

Asking for and giving explanations

You will often need to ask your teacher to explain things. The simplest way is to use **Why … ?**

> **Why** do I need to heat the liquid?
> **Why** are there no women poets on this list?
> **Why** won't this download?

Useful words

a break	a short period of time when you have a rest
sulphur	a yellow chemical that has an unpleasant smell
a revolution	an attempt by a group of people to change their country's government by using force
economics	the study of the way that money and industry are organized in a society
download	to move information to your computer from a bigger computer or network

Could you explain ... ? can be used to ask your teacher to explain something. Your teacher might use it to ask you to explain something too.

> **Could you explain** why the flame changes color?
> **Could you explain** what happens when the cell divides?
> **Could you explain** how to do this calculation?

To ask for a reason, use **What is the reason ... ?**

> **What is the reason** that birds fly south in winter?
> **What is the reason** for the change in temperature?
> **What is the reason** for Juliet's happiness?

To give an explanation, use **Because ...** .

> **Because** he forgot to charge his laptop, Eric couldn't show us his presentation.
> Your answer was not correct **because** you put the decimal point in the wrong place.
> **Because** he was really tired, Joe fell asleep in the library.

Useful words

a flame	the bright burning gas that comes from a fire
a cell	the smallest part of an animal or plant
divide	to separate into smaller parts
a calculation	when you find out a number or amount by using mathematics
presentation	a talk that gives information about something
a decimal point	the dot that you use when you write a number as a decimal

Explaining a problem

To explain a general problem, use **I've got a problem ...** or **I have a problem**.
Use the preposition **with** to talk about a thing that is causing your problem.

> **I have a problem** — I want to take a French class and a history class, but
> the classes are at the same time.
> **I have a problem** — this homework has to be done by tomorrow,
> but I don't have the books I need.
> **I have a problem with** my essay — it's too long, and I don't know what to
> cut out.
> **I have a problem with** my laptop.

If you need something for school but you don't have it, use **I don't have ...** .

> **I don't have** the books I need.
> **I don't have** Internet access at the moment.
> **I don't have** enough time to finish my essay.

If you are not able to do something, use **I can't ...** .

> **I can't** see the screen.
> **I can't** read his writing.
> **I can't** remember what we have to do for our next biology class.
> **I can't** find my notes.

Useful words

history	the study of events that happened in the past
an essay	a short piece of writing on a subject
cut something out	to remove something
access	when you are able or allowed to see or use information or equipment
a screen	a flat surface on a piece of electronic equipment, such as a television or a computer, where you see pictures or words
biology	the scientific study of living things
a note	something that you write down to remind yourself of something

Saying what you have to do

To tell people what you have to do, use **I have to ...** or **I need to ...** .

> **I have to** get to my chemistry class.
> **I have to** finish this essay by Monday.
> **I have to** study for my English test.

> **I need to** read this book.
> **I need to** buy a good dictionary.
> **I need to** ask the teacher to help me.

If something is important, you could use **It is important for me to ...** .

> **It is important for me to** pass this test.
> **It is important for me to** find my notes.
> **It is important for me to** work as hard as possible.

Asking if something is allowed or permitted

To ask your teacher if you can do something, use **Can I ... ?**

> **Can I** use the computer?
> **Can I** have a little longer to finish my homework?
> **Can I** use your dictionary?
> **Can I** borrow this book until next week?

Useful words

prepare	to get ready for something
dictionary	a book in which the words and phrases of a language are listed, together with their meanings
borrow	to use something that belongs to another person for a period of time and then return it

To ask if your teacher is happy for you to do something, use **Is it OK ... ?** or **Do you mind if ... ?**

> **Is it OK** to use a calculator?
> **Is it OK** to write in the margin?
> **Is it OK** if we work together?

> **Do you mind if** my essay's longer than you asked for?
> **Do you mind if** we take some chairs from your classroom?
> **Do you mind if** we look on the Internet?

You could also see if something is allowed by using **Are we allowed to ... ?**

> **Are we allowed to** use dictionaries?
> **Are we allowed to** work in pairs?
> **Are we allowed to** discuss the answers?

Asking for things

To ask for something, use **Can I ... ?** or **Could I ... ?** To be polite, use **please**.

> **Can I** have a handout, please?
> **Can I** borrow a ruler?
> **Can we** take a break?

> Please **could we** have more time?
> **Could I** have the key?
> **Could I** use your eraser?

Useful words

the margin	the empty space down the side of a page
a pair	two people who are doing something together
a handout	a piece of paper containing information that is given to people in a meeting or a class
a ruler	a long, flat object that you use for measuring things and for drawing straight lines
eraser	an object that is used for removing pencil marks

To ask if someone has something that you want, use **Do you have... ?**

> **Do you have** an extra textbook?
> **Do you have** any clay I can use?
> **Do you have** a copy of the new lab schedule?

If you need something, use **I need ...** .

> **I need** a red pen.
> **I need** some more paper.
> **I need** a calculator.

To ask someone to do something for you, use **Can you ... ?** or **Could you ... ?**

> **Can you** give us an example?
> **Can you** repeat the instructions?
> **Can you** pass me that book?

> **Could you** repeat that, please?
> **Could you** show me how to do it?
> **Could you** help me find the books I need?

Useful words

a textbook	a book containing facts about a particular subject that is used by people studying that subject
clay	a type of earth that is soft when it is wet and hard when it is dry, and is used for making things such as pots and bricks
a schedule	a plan that gives a list of the times when things happen
instructions	information on how to do something
repeat	to say something again

Saying what you like, dislike, prefer

To talk about things you like, use **I like ...** .

> **I like** working in the library.
> **I like** physics.
> **I like** Mrs. Kennedy's lessons.

For things you like a lot, use **I really like ...** or **I love ...** .

> **I really like** learning about computers.
> **I really like** our conversation classes.
> **I really like** the teachers here.

> **I love** learning about ancient history.
> **I love** the idea of going to college.
> **I love** discussing books in class.

For things you like doing, use **I enjoy ...** .

> **I enjoy** reading poetry.
> **I enjoy** studying languages.
> **I enjoy** meeting other students.

> **GOOD TO KNOW!**
> **Like/Enjoy + -ing**
> When **like** or **enjoy** are followed by a verb, the verb is usually in the -ing form.

To say what you do not like, use **I don't like ...** .

> **I don't like** physics.
> **I don't like** writing essays.
> **I don't like** doing homework.

Useful words

physics	the scientific study of things such as heat, light, and sound
ancient history	the study of people and life from a very long time ago
poetry	the form of literature that consists of poems

Talking about your plans

We often say **I'm going to ...** to talk about what we will do in the future.

> **I'm going to** drop French next year.
> **I'm going to** take a catering course.
> **We're going to** get our teacher a present.

You can also use **I'm planning to ...** .

> **I'm planning to** go to college.
> **I'm planning to** study Chinese next semester.
> **I'm planning to** be a teacher.

To ask someone about their plans, use **Are you going to ... ?**

> **Are you going to** study politics and government next year?
> **Are you going to** go to college?
> **Are you going to** go to summer school?

Useful words

drop	if you drop a subject, you stop studying it
catering	providing food and drinks for people
semester	a half of a school or college year
politics	the activities and ideas that are concerned with government

● Listen for

Here are some useful phrases you may hear at school.

Turn to page 10.
Open your books to page 56.
Get into pairs.
Work in groups of four.
Work with your partner.
Write the answers on a piece of paper.
Look it up in your dictionary.
Hand in your homework at the end of class.
Raise your hand if you know the answer.
Check your answers.
Make sure you read the questions carefully.
Put the equipment away when you finish using it.

Useful words

your partner	a person you are doing something with
look something up	to find a fact or piece of information by looking in a book or on a computer
hand something in	to take something to someone and give it to them

Listen to the conversation: Track 25

Craig is taking an evening class. His teacher is talking about a poem by William Shakespeare.

A Good evening, everyone. Could you turn to page 26 in your textbooks? Craig, could you tell us about this poem?

B It's a love poem.

A That's right. What do you think of it?

B I think it's very beautiful, but it's hard to understand. What does "temperate" mean?

A It means "gentle." Why do you think Shakespeare uses this word?

B Because it is a word that can be used for the weather, and he is comparing his love to a summer day.

A Very good, Craig. Do you think this is a good comparison?

B I think it is because he is saying that a summer day is very good, but his love is better. I don't understand the second verse, though.

A It's very difficult. I'd like you all to write down what you think it means. You have ten minutes.

B Are we allowed to work in pairs?

A Yes, if you like.

 Listen to more phrases and practise saying them: Track 26

Useful words

gentle	kind, mild, and calm
compare	to consider how things are different and how they are similar
a comparison	a study of the differences between two things
a verse	one of the groups of lines in a poem or a song

Numbers, dates, and time

Three, two, one... Go!

You will often need to use numbers in conversation. You will also need to talk about the time and dates. The phrases in this unit will help you to talk about all these things with confidence.

Numbers

For the unit of money that is written as $, use **... dollars** and for the smaller unit used with the dollar, use **... cents**. To say how much something costs using the unit of money that is written as €, use **... euros** and for the smaller unit used with the euro, use **... cents**. For the unit of money that is written as £, use **... pounds** and for the smaller unit used with the pound, use **... pence**.

> That'll be eighteen **dollars** and ninety-nine **cents**. ($18.99)
> It cost me sixty-five **euros** twenty. (€65.20)
> My ticket cost nine **pounds** fifty-nine. (£9.59)

To talk about how heavy something is using the units of measurement written as k and g, use **... kilos** and **... grams**. To talk about how heavy something is using the units of measurement written as lb. and oz., use **... pounds** and **... ounces**.

> You need three **pounds** of apples.
> The recipe says eight **ounces** of butter.
> I'd like two **kilos** of potatoes, please.
> Can I have half a **kilo** of tomatoes?

Useful words

cost	to have as a price
a bar	a small block of something
a recipe	a list of food and a set of instructions telling you how to cook something

numbers, dates, and time

To talk about how much liquid there is using the unit of measurement written as L or l, use **... liters**. For the unit of measurement written as gal, use **... gallons**.

> I put twenty **liters** of gas in the car.
> Could you buy a half **gallon** of milk, please?

The units of measurement written as km, m and cm, use **... kilometers, ... meters** and **... centimeters**. For the units of measurement written as m., yd., ft. and in., use **... miles, ... yards, ... feet,** and **... inches**.

> It's about eighty **miles** to Cardiff.
> He's over six **feet** tall.
> We're thirty **kilometers** from Madrid.
> I'm one **meter** sixty-six **centimeters** tall.

To talk about amounts as parts of a hundred (%), use **... percent**.

> Fifty-five **percent** of the students are from the U.S.
> The interest rate is two point five **percent**.

For talking about a temperature, written as °, use **... degrees**.

> It's over thirty-five **degrees** today.

Useful words

gas	the fuel which you use in cars and some other vehicles to make the engine go
milk	the white liquid which cows and some other animals produce, which people drink
wide	used to talk about how much something measures from one side to the other
vote	to show your choice officially at a meeting or in an election
interest rate	the percent of money that you pay if you borrow money, or the percent that you receive if you have money in the bank

To talk about the order in which something happens or comes, use **first, second, third,** etc ... .

> It's our **first** wedding anniversary today.
> This is my **second** trip to Provence.
> He finished in **third** place.

The time

Use **... o'clock** to say what time it is when the clock shows the exact hour.

> It finishes at eight **o'clock**.
> He got up this morning at five **o'clock**.
> It's one **o'clock** — time for lunch!
> It's four **o'clock** in the afternoon.

> **GOOD TO KNOW!**
> **Noon** is used to mean twelve o'clock in the middle of the day.
> **Midnight** is used to mean twelve o'clock in the middle of the night.

To say that it is thirty minutes or less after a particular hour, use **... past** or **after** ... .

> It's twenty-five **after** one.
> It's five **after** six.
> It's quarter **past** one.
> She's coming here at half **past** five.
> Class ends at three-**thirty**.

Useful words

a wedding	a marriage ceremony and the party that often takes place after the ceremony
an anniversary	a date that is remembered because something special happened on that date in an earlier year
a trip	a journey that you make to a particular place and back again
a race	a competition to see who is the fastest
get up	to get out of bed
lunch	the meal that you have in the middle of the day
quarter past or quarter after	used when you are telling the time to talk about fifteen minutes after an hour
half past or ... thirty	used when you are telling the time to talk about 30 minutes after an hour

To say that it is a particular number of minutes before a particular hour, use **... to ...** .

> It's twenty **to** one.
> It's ten **to** eight.
> I looked at my watch, and it was five **to** three.
> I'm leaving at quarter **to** one.

To find out the time now or the time that something starts, use **What time ... ?**

> **What time** is it?
> **What time**'s the next train to Providence?
> **What time** does it start?
> **What time** should we meet?

To say the time that something is happening, use **at ...** .

> It starts **at** seven o'clock.
> The train leaves **at** seven-thirty.
> I'll see you **at** half past three.
> Let's meet **at** quarter past five.

To say that something will happen at or before a particular time, use **by ...** .

> Can you be there **by** three o'clock?
> I have to leave **by** quarter to one.
> We have to finish this **by** quarter to one.

Useful words
quarter to   used when you are telling the time to talk about fifteen minutes
                       before an hour

● Listen for

Here are some important phrases you may hear and use to do with the time.

> Excuse me, do you have the time?
> I'm sorry, I'm not wearing a watch.
> It's probably about eleven.
> I'm late.
> I have to go. I'm late already.
> Did you get there on time?
> How much time do we have left?
> He should be here by now.

> The train for Paris leaves at 3:55.
> The 4:15 train to Dayton will depart from Platform Two.
> Flight number 307 for London is due to take off at 2:45.
> Flight 909 from Toronto is on time.
> The bus gets to Sydney at 9:10.

Saying how long

If you want to say that something will happen in so many minutes' time or in so many days' time, use **in ...** .

> I'll be back **in** twenty minutes.
> She'll be here **in** a week.
> He completed the exercise **in** only three minutes.
> I can probably do the job **in** an hour or two.

Useful words	
a watch	a small clock that you wear on your wrist
late	after the time that something should start or happen
on time	not late or early
depart	to leave
due	expected to happen or arrive at a particular time
take off	used for saying that a plane leaves the ground and starts flying
complete	to finish a task
an exercise	an activity that you do in order to practice a skill

To ask how much time something lasts or how much time you need for something, use **How long ... ?**

> **How long**'s the movie?
> **How long** does the meeting usually last?
> **How long** will the tour take?
> **How long** will it take you to get there?

To say how much time something is needed to do something, use **It takes ...** .

> **It takes** five minutes to make.
> **It takes** about forty minutes to cook.
> **It took** two hours to drive to the lake.

The seasons

To say which season, (spring, summer, autumn, or winter), something happens or happened in, use **in ...** .

> The weather is really beautiful **in** spring.
> We don't go camping **in** winter.
> They got married **in** the summer of 2009.

Useful words

a meeting	an event in which a group of people come together to discuss things or make decisions
a tour	a trip to an interesting place or around several interesting places
cook	to prepare and heat food
weather	the temperature and conditions outside, for example if it is raining, hot, or windy
camping	the activity of staying somewhere in a tent
get married	to legally become husband and wife in a special ceremony

To make it clear which spring, summer, etc. you are talking about, use **last ...** , **this ...**, or **next ...** .

> We're going to Oregon **this** summer.
> I'm going to South Africa **this** winter.
> It was very cold **last** winter.
> She's expecting her baby **next** spring.

The months of the year

To say which month of the year something happens or happened in, use **in ...** .

> My birthday is **in** August.
> We'll probably take our vacation **in** May.
> I visited some friends in Rome **in** September.
> We're going to the mountains **in** August.

To make it clear which January or February, etc. you are talking about, use **last ...** , **this ...** , or **next ...** .

> Where did you take your vacation **last** June?
> I'm hoping to go to Peru **next** July.

If you want to say which part of a month something happens in, use **at the start of ...**, **in the middle of ...**, or **at the end of ...** .

> She begins school **at the start of** September.
> Summer vacation starts **at the end of** June.
> They're leaving **in the middle of** November.

Useful words

expect a baby	to have a baby growing inside you
a birthday	the day of the year that you were born
a mountain	a very high area of land with steep sides

Dates

To say what the date is, use **the first/second, etc. of March/November, etc.**
or **March/November, etc. first/second, etc.**

>It's **the first of July** today.
>Tomorrow's **the tenth of January**.
>Today's **December third**.
>It's **March fifth**.

To say what date something is happening or happened on, use **on ...** before
the date.

>He was born **on** the fourteenth of February, 1990.
>He died **on** April twenty-third, 1616.
>Barbara and Tomek got married **on** May fifteenth.
>Where do you think you'll be **on** the twentieth of October?

>**GOOD TO KNOW!**
>To ask what the date is, use **What's today's date?**

The days of the week

To say what day of the week it is, use **Today's...** or **It's ...** .

>"What day is it?" "**It's** Thursday."
>**Today's** Wednesday, isn't it?
>Great! **It's** Saturday.

Useful words
be born   to come out of your mother's body and start life
die   to stop living

When saying which day something happens or will happen, use **on ...** .

> I'm going to Houston **on** Sunday.
> It's my birthday **on** Tuesday.
> We'll see them **on** Wednesday.
> I don't work **on** Fridays.

To say what time of a particular day something happens, use **on ... morning/ afternoon/evening/night**.

> I'm going to the garage **on Tuesday morning**.
> I'll see you **on Friday afternoon**.
> There was a good movie on TV **on Sunday evening**.
> What are you doing **on Saturday night**?

To say that you do something all Mondays/Saturdays, etc. use **every ...** .

> We call her **every** Monday.
> He plays golf **every** Saturday.
> I used to see them **every** Friday.
> They go to the same café **every** Saturday morning.

To say that you do something one Wednesday/week, etc. and then not the next Wednesday/week, etc., and that it continues in this way, use **every other ...** .

> He has the children **every other** weekend.
> We play football **every other** Saturday.

Useful words

a garage	a place where you can have your car repaired
golf	a game in which you use long sticks to hit a small, hard ball into holes

To make it clear which Monday/Wednesday, etc. you are talking about, use **last ...** , **this ...**, or **next ...** .

> It's our wedding anniversary **this** Friday.
> I'm going on vacation **this** Tuesday.
> I sent you the pictures **last** Friday.
> Would **next** Friday be better for you?

If you want to ask what day something is happening, use **What day ... ?**

> **What day**'s the meeting? Is it Tuesday?
> Do you know **what day** he's coming?

To say what day it is today, use **It's ...** .

> **It's** Tuesday.
> **It's** Friday.

To talk about a particular time the day after today, use **tomorrow ...** .

> I'm seeing her **tomorrow** evening.
> I've got to be up early **tomorrow** morning.
> We're going to a concert **tomorrow** night.

Useful words
up   not in bed

To talk about a particular time the day before today, use **yesterday ...** .

> It happened **yesterday** morning.
> I saw him **yesterday** afternoon.

GOOD TO KNOW!
To talk about the night that belonged to yesterday, use **last night**.

To say when something happened, use **... ago**.

> She called me a week **ago**.
> They left ten days **ago**.
> He was born three years **ago**.

To say how long something has been happening, use **for ...** .

> It's been raining **for** five days.
> I haven't seen them **for** three weeks.
> They haven't spoken to each other **for** months.
> I've been waiting here **for** hours.
> We've been living here **for** ten months.
> I haven't seen her **for** a week.

GOOD TO KNOW!
Another way to say "for a long time" is **for ages**.

Useful words
it rains   water falls from the clouds in small drops

● Listen for

Here are some important phrases you may hear and use to do with dates, months of the year, and days of the week.

> When's your birthday?
> It's my birthday today!
> It's my parents' wedding anniversary today.
> When are you getting married?
> When are you going on vacation?
> When do you start classes?
> When are you going to Rio?
> When do you come back from Rio?
> When is the baby due?
> When was Carlo born?
> When do you play tennis?
> Which days are you free?
> Is Saturday good for you?
> How about this Saturday?
> I'm afraid I'm busy on Saturday.
> Which month is Lena's birthday in?
> Which months are the hottest?

Useful words
busy   doing something, so that you are not free to do anything else

Listen to the conversation: Track 27

Emma and Katie are arranging to see each other.

A We could meet up for coffee if you like. What are you doing this Thursday?

B Thursday is no good, I'm afraid. I'm having dinner with my boss and her husband. What about next Thursday? Are you free that afternoon?

A Oh, no, I'm away then — I'm going to be in Mexico City.

B Oh, right. When do you come back?

A On July eleventh.

B Well, how about the Thursday after you get back — July fourteenth?

A That's a possibility. The only problem is, I have a meeting in the afternoon.

B How long will your meeting last?

A It'll probably finish by five o'clock. It only takes ten minutes to get downtown from my office. I could meet you at the café at around 5:30.

B OK, great. Let's say Dino's Café at 5:30.

A Perfect!

 Listen to more phrases and practice saying them: Track 28

All the phrases by function ...

So, to sum up ...

This unit helps you find quickly all the phrases you have learned. You will find all the phrases that are used for the same function in one place under a heading.

Contents

Agreeing and disagreeing

To agree to do something or give someone something, use **Yes** or **OK**. To make **Yes** sound more enthusiastic, add **of course**.

> "Will you come with me?" "**Yes**."
> "Could you help me with my bags?" "**Yes, of course**."
> "Can I have ice cream?" "**Yes**."

> "Can you cook dinner tonight?" "**OK**, if you like."
> "Will you drive?" "**OK**."
> "Can I borrow your pen?" "**OK**."

To say you will not do something or give someone something, use **No**.

> "Could you give me a lift?" "**No**, sorry, I don't have time."
> "Will you pay for the coffee?" "**No**, it's your turn."

To agree with someone's opinion, use **I agree** or **You're right.** If you want to say who you agree with, use **with**.

> "This is a great restaurant." "**I agree**. We come here a lot."
> **I agree with** Nigel.
> I completely **agree with you**!

> "We'll be late if we don't hurry." "**You're right** — let's go!"
> I think **you're right**.
> Matt**'s right**.

If you do not agree with someone's opinion, you can use **I don't think so.**

> "The food here's great, isn't it?" "**I don't think so.** My soup is much too salty."
> "Pierre's really nice, isn't he?" "**I don't think so.** He never speaks to me."
> "Traveling by train is really relaxing." "**I don't think so.** I prefer to fly."

Apologizing

To apologize, use **I'm sorry ...** or **Sorry ...** .

> **I'm sorry**. I've forgotten your name.
> **I'm sorry**, I forgot to bring those figures with me.
> **I'm sorry** I'm late.

> **Sorry**. I have to leave now.
> **Sorry**, I didn't hear what you were saying.
> **Sorry**. I didn't introduce you.

If you have to tell someone that there is a problem or that something bad has happened, start your sentence with **I'm afraid ...** .

> **I'm afraid** I'm going to be late.
> **I'm afraid** I can't come tonight.
> **I'm afraid** there's a problem with your order.

If someone says sorry to you, you can make them feel better by saying **It doesn't matter** or **Don't worry about it.**

> "I'm sorry. I spilled your drink." "**It doesn't matter**."
> "Sorry we're late." "**It doesn't matter** — I just got here myself."

> "Sorry I forgot your birthday." "**Don't worry about it**."
> "I'm afraid the handle came off the door." "**Don't worry about it** –
>   it happens all the time."

A more informal way to tell someone that something does not matter is **No problem** or **That's OK**.

> "Sorry I can't come to your party." "**No problem.** I understand."
> "We ate all the food." "**No problem**. I'm not hungry."

> "Sorry about the noise." "**That's OK**. It didn't bother me."
> "I didn't bring a coat." "**That's OK**. I can lend you one."

Asking for and giving explanations

The simplest way to ask for an explanation is to use **Why ... ?**

> **Why** do I need to save these files?
> **Why** are there no women poets on this list?
> **Why** can't we leave now?

Could you explain ... ? can be used to ask someone to explain something.

> **Could you explain** why the door's locked?
> **Could you explain** what happens when the power goes off?
> **Could you explain** how to do this?

To give an explanation, use **Because ...** .

> **Because** he was working in Paris at that time, Tim missed the wedding.
> Your answer was not correct **because** you put the decimal point in the
>   wrong place.
> **Because** he was not able to drive any more, my uncle sold his car.

Asking for information

To ask for information, use the question words **Where ... ?**, **When ... ?**,
Why ... ?, **Who ... ?**, **Which ... ?**, **What ... ?**, and **How ... ?**

> **Where** is your office?
> **Where** do you work?

> **When** did you meet Olga?
> **When** is his presentation?

Why did you decide to become a teacher?
Why did you leave Tokyo?

Who did you see last time?
Who is your doctor?

Which brand do you recommend?
Which batteries do I need for my ereader?

What's the name of the hotel?
What's the landlord's address?

How can we find a plumber?
How do I turn the computer on?

Use **Tell me ...** for general questions about someone's life.

Tell me about your family.
Tell me about yourself.
Tell me about your job.

To ask someone to describe someone or something use **What's ... like?**

What's your class **like**?
What's his new apartment **like**?
What's your hotel **like**?

We often start questions that ask for information with **Is ... ?**

Is it expensive?
Is it far from the city center?
Is breakfast included?

To ask questions about something, especially in a store, use **Is this ... ?** or **Is it ... ?**

Is this the only model you have?
Is this the biggest size?
Are these the only colors you have?

Is it made of real leather?
Is it big enough for four people?
Is it free?

To ask if a place has something, use **Is there ... ?**, or **Are there any ... ?**

Is there a hair dryer in the room?
Is there a TV?
Is there a pool?

Are there any good schools near here?
Are there any rules about having guests?
Are there any more blankets?

You could also use **Does ... have ... ?**

Does the apartment **have** central heating?
Does the hotel **have** a swimming pool?
Does it **have** a garden?

To ask how to do something, use **How do you ... ?**

How do you get to the old part of town?
How do you buy tickets?
How do you know which bus to take?

To ask about time, use **What time ... ?**

What time's dinner?
What time does he get home?
What time do we have to leave in the morning?

To ask about prices, use **How much ... ?**

How much is a double room?
How much is the rent?
How much do you charge for Internet service?

To ask about the time that something will take, use **How long ... ?**

> **How long** does the tour last?
> **How long** is the boat trip?
> **How long** does it take to get there?

Asking if something is allowed or permitted

To ask if something is allowed or permitted, use **Can I ... ?**

> **Can I** see the room?
> **Can I** pay by credit card?
> **Can we** camp here?

To check if you can do something, use **Is it OK to ... ?**

> **Is it OK to** use the washing machine?
> **Is it OK to** have guests?
> **Is it OK to** ask questions?

To make sure you will not upset someone, use **Do you mind if ... ?**

> **Do you mind if** I park my car here for a moment?
> **Do you mind if** I leave my suitcase here for five minutes?
> **Do you mind if** we look at the rooms before we decide?

A slightly informal way of asking if something is allowed or permitted is **Is it OK to ... ?**

> **Is it OK to** look inside the box?
> **Is it OK to** try those?
> **Is it OK to** take the MP3 player out of its box?

Asking for things

To ask for something, use **Can I have ... ?** or **Could I have ... ?** To be very polite, use **please** at the beginning or end of the question.

> **Can I have** two tickets, **please**?
> **Can I have** your travel guide for a minute?
> **Can I have** an audio guide, **please**?

> **Could I have** the key to my room, please?
> **Could I have** a receipt, please?
> **Please could I have** two more towels?

To say what you want, use **I'd like ...** .

> **I'd like** a double room, please.
> **I'd like** to stay three nights.
> **I'd like** an apartment near the university.

To describe the thing you want, use **I'm looking for ...** or **I want ...** .

> **I'm looking for** a room in a house.
> **I'm looking for** a place to rent.
> **We're looking for** a house with four bedrooms.

> **I want** a house with a large garden.
> **I want** to rent a house for six months.
> **I want** a room with a view of the ocean.

If it is important for you to have something, you can use **I need ...** .

> **I need** the address of the museum.
> **She needs** two more tickets.
> **We need** a guide who can speak English.

To ask if a shop sells the thing you want, use **Do you sell ... ?**

> **Do you sell** light bulbs?
> **Do you sell** fruit?
> **Do you sell** newspapers?

To ask if a store sells the thing you want or if someone has the thing you want, use **Do you have ... ?**

> **Do you have** any strawberries?
> **Do you have** an extra textbook?
> **Do you have** a copy of the new timetable?

When you have decided what you want to buy in a store, use **I'll have ...** or **I'll take ...** .

> **I'll have** strawberry ice cream.
> **I'll have** a salad.
> **I'll have** half a pound of ham.

> **I'll take** these two postcards.
> **I'll take** the blue ones.
> **I'll take** two pineapples.

If you are asking someone if they can do something for you, use **Can you ... ?** or **Could you ... ? Could you ... ?** is slightly more polite and formal than **Can you ...?** To be very polite, use **please**

> **Can you** tell me what the hours are?
> **Can you** give me directions to the childrens museum?
> **Can you please** show me where we are on this map?

> **Could you** show me the room, **please**?
> **Could you** get someone to fix the window?
> **Could you** call a taxi for me, **please**?

Can I ... ? is also used when you are asking if something you want to do is possible. If you want to be very polite, you can use **Is it possible to ... ?**

> **Can I** see the dentist this morning?
> **Can I** talk to a nurse?
> **Can I** drive while I'm taking this medicine?

> **Is it possible to** see a different doctor?
> **Is it possible to** get an earlier appointment?
> **Is it possible to** meet the surgeon before my operation?

Attracting someone's attention

When you are asking for information you may need to get someone's attention before you can ask them a question. To do this, first say **Excuse me**.

> **Excuse me**, is the modern art museum near here?
> **Excuse me**, do you know what time the gardens open?
> **Excuse me**, where can I buy a ticket?

Complaining

A simple way to start a sentence explaining what is wrong is to use **It's ...** .

> **It's** very cold in my room.
> **It's** too expensive.
> **It's** not big enough.

To talk about an event or an activity that is now over, use **It was ...** .

> **It was** really expensive.
> **It was** a waste of money.
> **It was** difficult to find.

To talk about something that should not be there, use **There's ...** .

> **There's** too much noise.
> **There's** dirt all over the floor.
> **There's** a hole in the wall.

If you think you should have something that you do not have, use **There isn't ...** .

> **There isn't** any hot water.
> **There isn't** anyplace to keep my bike.
> **There isn't** enough room for all my books.

If something is not good enough, use **I'm not happy with ...** .

> **I'm not happy with** the food.
> **I'm not happy with** my room.
> **I'm not happy with** the way the place is cleaned.

Congratulating someone

To show that you are pleased that something good has happened to someone, use **Congratulations!**

> **Congratulations** on your new job!
> **Congratulations** on the birth of your son!
> You passed? **Congratulations!**

To show that you think someone has done something very well, use **Nice going!**

> **Nice going**, Mercedes!
> "I got that job, by the way." "**Nice going!** That's great!"
> "Look, I straightened up all those papers." "**Nice going!**"

Danger and emergencies

To ask for help because you are in danger, shout **Help!**

> **Help!** I can't swim!
> **Help!** The building's on fire!

To tell someone that they are in danger, shout **Look out!** or say **Be careful!**

> **Look out!** There's a car coming!
> **Look out!** It's falling!

> **Be careful** on those steps!
> **Be careful!** It's icy outside.

Describing people and things

Start general descriptions of things with **It's ...** and of people with **He's/She's ...** .

> **It's** gold with three diamonds.
> **It's** a ladies' watch.
> **It's** a green suitcase with wheels.

> **He's** five years old.
> **She's** eight.
> **He was** about sixty.

Use **It's made of ...** to say what something is made of.

> **It's made of** leather.
> It's a small bag, and **it's made of** velvet.
> The beads are bright blue, and **they're made of** glass.

Use **He/She has ...** to talk about what someone looks like.

> **She has** short blond hair.
> **He has** a beard.
> **She has** a small mouth.

To talk about someone's clothes, use **He's/She's wearing ...** .

> **She's wearing** jeans and a green T-shirt.
> **She's wearing** an orange blouse.
> **He's wearing** a black jacket.

Encouraging someone

To encourage someone to go somewhere more quickly or to do something more quickly, use **Hurry up!**

> **Hurry up!** We've got to be there in ten minutes!
> **Hurry up!** We're late already!

To encourage someone to go somewhere or to do something more quickly, you can also use **Come on!**

> **Come on**, Helena, or we'll be late!
> **Come on!** We're going to miss our train!
> **Come on!** We haven't got all day!
> **Come on!** Get into the pool. The water's great!

To encourage someone to do something, you can use **Go for it! Go for it!** is informal.

> "I'm thinking of applying for that job." "**Go for it!**"
> "I've decided I want to run a marathon." "**Go for it!**"
> "I'd like to go and see Paolo in New York." "**Go for it!**"

Explaining a problem

To explain a general problem, use **I have a problem ...** . Use the preposition **with** to talk about a thing that is causing your problem.

> **I have a problem**. I want to study French and Italian, but the classes are at the same time.
> **I have a problem**. This homework has to be done by tomorrow, but I don't have all the books I need.
> **I have a problem with** my presentation. It's far too long, and I don't know what to cut out.
> **I have a problem with** my ereader.

If you are asking somebody for help, you will need to be able to describe the problem. Use **There's ...** to say what the problem is.

> **There's** a noise coming from the engine.
> **There are** mice in the kitchen.
> **There's** water all over the floor.

If the problem is that you do not have something you need, use **There isn't ...** or **I don't have ...** .

> **There isn't** any soap in the bathroom.
> **There isn't** enough food for everyone.
> **There aren't** any towels in my room.

> **I don't have** her address.
> **She doesn't have** enough money.
> **He doesn't have** a car.

For some problems, you can use **I have ...** .

> **I have** a problem.
> **I have** a flat tire.
> **I have** too much work.

If the problem is that you are not able to do something, use **I can't ...** .

> **I can't** drive.
> **We can't** open the bedroom door.
> **I can't** find my keys.

If you want to say that you do not understand something, use **I don't understand ...** .

> **I don't understand** what he's saying.
> **I don't understand** the instructions.
> **I don't understand** how to use this phone.

Expressing opinions

To express your opinions, use **I think ...** .

> **I think** Sonia's right.
> I really **think** it's too late to go to the movies.
> **I think** it's a great idea.

If you do not think something is true, use **I don't think ...** .

> **I don't think** Marc's coming.
> **I don't think** we should stay much longer.
> **I don't think** the restaurant is open on Mondays.

If you want to ask other people if they think something is good or bad, use **What do you think of ... ?**

> **What do you think of** his latest movie?
> **What do you think of** this idea?
> **What do you think of** Mira's new car?

To ask someone if they think something is a good idea, use **What do you think about ... ?**

> **What do you think about** going out for dinner tonight?
> **What do you think about** inviting Eva?
> **What do you think about** having a party this weekend?

If you are trying to choose between two or more things, and you want an opinion from the person you are with, use **Which ... ?**

> **Which** one do you like?
> **Which** dress should I buy?
> **Which** skirt fits best?

Expressing surprise

A simple way to show that you are surprised by what someone has said is to use **Really?**

> "Zack is leaving?" "**Really?** Why?"
> "I don't think it's a very good school." "**Really?** I was very impressed by it."
> "I'm really bad at math." "**Really?** I can't believe that!"

A stronger way to show that you are surprised by what someone has said is to say **That's incredible!** or **That's amazing!**

> You ran twenty miles in two and a half hours? **That's incredible!**
> So he works a sixty-hour week? **That's incredible!**
>
> She spent 2,000 dollars on a jacket? **That's amazing!**
> You cooked for sixty people? **That's amazing!**

Expressing sympathy

The most common way to show that you are sad for someone when something bad has happened is to use **I'm sorry to hear ...** .

> I'm so **sorry to hear** that your mother died.
> **I'm sorry to hear** that Charlie has lost his job, Sara.
> **I'm sorry to hear** you didn't get the job.

To show that you are sorry when something slightly bad or disappointing has happened, use **It's a shame ...** .

> **It's a shame** you couldn't come with us last night.
> **It's a shame** she didn't graduate after all that hard work.
> **It's a shame** so few people came to the concert.

Hellos and goodbyes

Use **Hello** as a general greeting. It is polite to say **Hello** to anyone in any situation.

> **Hello,** Jorge.
> **Hello,** Dr. Huddlestone.

Use **Hi** in informal situations, for example when you are meeting friends.

> **Hi**, how are things with you?
> **Hi**, how are you doing?
> Oh **hi,** Adam. I didn't know you were coming.

Use **Good morning, Good afternoon,** or **Good evening** in slightly more formal situations, for instance if you meet a neighbor, or when you see people at work.

> **Good morning,** everyone. Today we are going to learn how to form questions.
> **Good afternoon,** Mr. Kowalski.

Use **Goodbye** when you leave someone.

> **Goodbye,** Dwight. Have a safe trip.

Goodbye is often shortened to **Bye**.

> **Bye,** everyone!

Use **Goodnight** when you are going to bed, or if someone else is going to bed.

> **Goodnight,** everyone. See you in the morning.

See you is an informal way of saying goodbye to someone you know you will see again.

> OK, I need to go now. **See you!**
> **See you** tomorrow!
> **See you** on Monday!

If someone has come to a place for the first time, you could say **Welcome!**

> **Welcome!** I'm so pleased you could come.
> **Welcome** to Blakey Publishing.
> **Welcome** to Vancouver!

Introducing people

If you want to introduce someone to someone else, use **This is ...** . To introduce a group of people, use **These are ...** .

> **This is** my husband, Richard.
> **This is** Medina, my friend from school.

> **These are** my children, Andrew, Gordon, and Emma.
> **These are** my parents.

> **GOOD TO KNOW!**
> When you are introduced to someone, you can just say **Hello**, or in a slightly more formal situation, say **Pleased to meet you** or **Nice to meet you**.

Making arrangements

To make an arrangement, use **We can ...** .

> **We can** have lunch in town.
> **We can** meet after work.
> **We can** go together.

To explain an arrangement, use **I'll ...** .

> **I'll** meet you outside the theater.
> **I'll** pick you up at seven.
> **I'll** text you when I'm ready.

To ask someone about the place they want to meet, use **Where ... ?**

> **Where** do you want to meet?
> **Where** should we go to eat?
> **Where** would you like to eat?

To ask someone about the time they want to meet, use **When ... ?** or **What time ... ?**

> **When** should we eat?
> **When** do you want to meet for dinner?
> **When** do you want to have dinner?

> **What time** should we meet?
> **What time** would you like to meet?
> **What time** would you like to eat?

To check if someone is happy with an arrangement, use **Is ... OK?**

> **Is** eight o'clock **OK?**
> **Is** it **OK** to bring a pizza?
> **Is** it **OK** to bring Charlie?

To ask what the best arrangement is, use **Is it better to ... ?**

> **Is it better to** meet outside the restaurant?
> **Is it better to** make a reservation?
> **Is it better to** arrive early?

Making suggestions

One easy way of making suggestions is to use **We could ...** .

> **We could** ask Paul to join us.
> **We could** meet another time.
> **We could** meet at the Café de la Poste.

To suggest what someone else can do, use **You could ...** .

> **You could** go on a tour of the city.
> **You could** ask Jan to show you around town .
> **You could** take the children to the fair.

If you are eager to do something, you could say **Let's ...** .

> **Let's** buy some flowers.
> **Let's** get the expensive one. It will be much better.
> **Let's** buy new bedding.

If you want to make a suggestion and see if other people agree with you, use **Should we ... ?**

> **Should we** see what Valerio wants to do?
> **Should we** order a pizza?
> **Should we** ask Suri if she wants to come with us?

If you have an idea about something you could do, use **How about ... ?**

> **How about** going swimming?
> **How about** asking for some time off from work?
> **How about** sending him a text?

Making sure you've understood

If you do not understand what someone has said, use **I don't understand.**

> Sorry, **I don't understand.**
> **I don't understand** what you said.
> Could you please repeat that, please? **I didn't understand**.

You can ask for help with understanding by using **Would you mind ... ?**

> **Would you mind** speaking more slowly?
> **Would you mind** repeating that?
> **Would you mind** speaking in English?

To check the meaning of a word, use **What does ... mean?**

> **What does** "fragile" **mean**?
> **What does** "end up" **mean**?
> **What does** "out of order" **mean**?

> **GOOD TO KNOW!**
> If you do not hear what someone has said and you want them
> to repeat it, use **Excuse me**.

Please and thank you

When asking for something from someone, use **please**.

> Three oranges, **please**.
> A large apple pie, **please**.
> Could you give these to Andrew, **please**?
> Could I borrow this chair, **please**?
> Could you **please** clean up now?

To say that you would like something that someone has offered you, use **Yes, please.**

> "Would you like some more coffee?" "**Yes, please**."
> "Can I help you with those bags?" "Oh, **yes, please**."
> "Would you like me to mail this for you?" "**Yes, please**."

To thank someone, use **Thank you** or **Thanks**. **Thanks** is slightly informal.

> **Thank you** for all your help, Sally.
> **Thank you** very much for coming here tonight.
> "Here's a little birthday present." "**Thank you!**"
> "You look beautiful in that dress." "**Thank you**, Judy."

> **GOOD TO KNOW!**
> To make **Thank you** or **Thanks** stronger, use **very much**.

> "Have a cup of coffee." "**Thanks**, Mike."
> "I love your new haircut." "**Thanks**, Juliana."
> Hey, **thanks** for helping out this weekend, Anne. I really appreciate it.
> **Thanks very much** for all those books you gave us. It was very nice of you.

> **GOOD TO KNOW!**
> People often say something extra after saying **thank you** or **thanks**.
> For example, they may say **I appreciate it** or **You were a great help**.
> They sometimes say **It was very nice of you**.

To accept someone's thanks, use **You're welcome** or **Not at all.**

> "Thank you very much for all your help, John. We appreciate it."
> "**You're welcome**."
> "Thanks for dinner last night. It was really lovely." "**You're welcome**.
>   Any time."

> "Thanks for looking after the children on Saturday — that was a great
>   help, Lucia." "**Not at all**."
> "Thank you for lending me the book. I loved it." "**Not at all**."

Another way of accepting someone's thanks is to use **It's my pleasure** or
My pleasure. This is a slightly more formal way of accepting thanks.

> "Thank you for the lovely gifts." "**It's my pleasure**."
> "Thank you very much for your check. It was very kind of you, Maya."
>   "**It's my pleasure**."

> "Thank you, Simone." "**My pleasure.**"
> "Thank you, Ben. You've been a great help." "**My pleasure.**"

Another way of accepting thanks from a person that you know is to use
No problem.

> "Thanks for looking after Rosie — it was a great help." "**No problem**."
> "Thanks for the invitation." "**No problem**."

Saying what you have to do

To tell people what you have to do, use **I have to ...** or **I've got to ...** .

> **I have to** make a call.
> **I have to** stay home tonight.
> **We have to** be there at eight o'clock.

> **I've got to** buy a present for Max.
> **I've got to** get a new toothbrush.
> **I've got to** replace my laptop.

To ask what someone has to do, use **Do you have to ...?**

> **Do you have to** give them an answer today?
> **Do you have to** go now?
> **Do we have to** bring something?

When you want to say that you should something, use **I should ...** .

> **I should** call Anne.
> **You should** come and visit us.
> **I should** give you my cellphone number.

You could also use **I need to ...** .

> **I need to** get some apples.
> **I need to** buy a tent.
> **I need to** get a new pair of glasses.

If something is important, you could use **It is important for me to ...** .

> **It is important for me to** pass this exam.
> **It is important for me to** find my notes.
> **It is important for me to** work as hard as possible.

Saying what you like, dislike, prefer

To talk about what you like, use **I like ...** .

> **I like** small hotels.
> **I like** campsites in the mountains.
> **I like** this house.

If you like something very much, use **I really like ...** or **I love ...** .

> **I really like** living here.
> **I really like** your sofa.
> **I really like** being so close to work.

> **I love** modern furniture.
> **I love** the peace of the countryside.
> **I love** living on my own.

If you like something, but not in a strong way, use **I sort of like ...** .

> **I sort of like** going to the movies.
> **I sort of like** the ballet.
> **I sort of like** exploring new places.

For things you like doing, use **I enjoy ...** .

> **I enjoy** reading poetry.
> **I enjoy** studying languages.
> **I enjoy** meeting other students.

If you do not like something, use **I don't like ...** .

>I **don't like** this hotel.
>I **don't like** living with my brother.
>I **don't like** this building.

To say very strongly that you do not like something, use **I hate ...** .

>I **hate** being late.
>I **hate** horror movies.
>I **hate** traveling by subway.

If you want to say that you like one thing more than another, use **I prefer ...** .
If you want to talk about the thing you like less, use **to**.

>I **prefer** living near the beach **to** living in the city.
>I **prefer** living alone.
>I **prefer** this town **to** my hometown.

You can also use **I like ... more than ...** .

>I **like** the yellow one **more than** the red one.
>I **like** the plastic cups **more than** the glass ones.
>I **like** orange juice **more than** apple juice.

Saying what you want to do

To talk about what you would like to do, use **I'd like to ...** or **I want to ...** .

>**I'd like to** talk to him about his trip to Canada.
>**I'd like to** meet your family.
>**We'd like to** take you out for dinner.

>I **want to** leave by 5:00 this afternoon.
>I **want to** speak to her as soon as possible.
>I **want to** invite you all for dinner.

If you know that you do not want to do something, use **I don't want to ...** .

> **I don't want to** stay in this room.
> **I don't want to** leave my car here.
> **We don't want to** go to the hotel without our luggage.

If you are very eager to do something, use **I'd really like to ...** or **I'd love to ...** .

> **I'd really like to** see the Great Wall of China.
> **I'd really like to** take the children to the beach.
> **I'd really like to** take some pictures.

> **I'd love to** go to the movies.
> **I'd love to** go hiking in the mountains.
> **I'd love to** visit the palace.

Use **I'd prefer to ...** when you want to do one thing and not another.

> **I'd prefer to** go to a local hospital.
> **I'd prefer to** see a female doctor.
> **I'd prefer to** drive there.

You can talk about things that it is important for you to do by using **I need to ...** .

> **I need to** buy a dictionary.
> **You need to** see a doctor.
> **I need to** go to the pharmacy.

Talking about your health

After saying hello to someone, especially someone we know, we usually ask about their health, by saying **How are you?**

> Hello, Jan. **How are you?**
> It's great to see you, Anna. **How are you?**

> **GOOD TO KNOW!**
> To answer that question, use **I'm fine, thanks** or **I'm good thanks.** .
> If you are not well, you could say **Not great, really** or **Not too good, actually.**

If you need to describe a medical problem, you can use **I have ...** .

> **I have** a temperature.
> **I have** a cold.
> **I have** asthma.

If you want to say which part of your body hurts, use **My ... hurts**.

> **My** back **hurts**.
> **His** foot **hurts**.
> **My** neck **hurts**.

If the pain you have is an ache, you can say which part of your body it is in by using **I have ... ache**.

> **I have** a head**ache**.
> **I have** a stomach**ache**.
> **She has a** tooth**ache**.

You can talk about more general problems by using **I feel ...** .

> **I feel** tired all the time.
> **I feel** sick.
> **I feel** like I'm getting a cold.

Talking about your plans

To tell people about your plans, use **I'm going to ...** or **I'll ...** .

> **I'm going to** call him.
> **I'm going to** tell him I can't come.
> **I'm going to** have lunch with Ted.

> **I'll** be staying for a week.
> **I'll** pay the rent in advance.
> **We'll** arrive in the evening.

To ask someone about their plans, use **Are you going to ... ?** or **Will you ... ?**

> **Are you going to** go to the concert?
> **Are you going to** look for a new job?
> **Are you going to** take a taxi home?

> **Will you** spend all day at the museum?
> **Will you** have time to see the gardens?
> **Will you** take your umbrella with you?

You can tell people about your plans using **I'm planning to ...** .

> **I'm planning to** buy an apartment near the river.
> **I'm planning to** rent a room in a colleague's house.
> **I'm planning to** move to London.

To talk about what you're thinking of doing, use **I'm thinking of ...** .

> **I'm thinking of** going to the mall tomorrow.
> **I'm thinking of** going shopping in New York City.
> **I'm thinking of** buying a new car.

For something you would like to do, but that is not certain, use **I hope to ...** .

> **I hope to** find something for under 20 dollars.
> **I hope to** buy a cheap sofa.
> **We hope to** find a present for Phil.

Talking about yourself

When you are talking to people, you will probably want to tell them some things about you. To say what your name is, use **I'm ...** or, in a more formal situation, **My name's ...** .

> Hi, **I'm** Tariq. I'm a friend of Susie's.
> **I'm** Paul. I'm your teacher for this week.
>
> **My name's** Johann.
> **My name's** Yuko. I'm Kazuo's sister.

If you want to say how old you are, use **I'm ...** . You can just say a number, or you can add **... years old** after the number.

> **I'm** twenty-two.
> **I'm** thirty-seven **years old**.

To give general information about yourself, use **I'm ...** .

> **I'm** a friend of Paolo's.
> **I'm** married with two children.
> **I'm** interested in old cars.

To talk about your work, use **I'm a ...** with the name of a job, or **I work ...** to say something more general about what you do.

> **I'm a** doctor.
> **I'm a** bus driver.

> **I work** for an oil company.
> **I work** in Paris.
> **I work** as a translator.

> **GOOD TO KNOW!**
> If you want to ask someone what their job is, use **What do you do?**

To talk about where you live, use **I live ...** or **I'm from ...** . **I'm from ...** is also used to talk about where you were born and lived as a child, even if you do not live there now.

> **I live** in Wales.
> **We live** near Moscow.

> **I'm from** Chicago, but I live in Phoenix now.
> **We're from** Atlanta.

Grammar

Irregular verbs

Regular verbs form the simple present tense for he/she/it by adding **-s**, the present participle by adding **-ing**, and the simple past tense and the past participle by adding **-ed** to the base form.

walk   walks   walking   walked   walked

Irregular verbs do not follow the same pattern. Here are some of the most useful irregular verbs.

base verb	he/she/it simple present	present participle (-ing form)	simple past	past participle
be	is	being	was/were	been
beat	beats	beating	beat	beaten
become	becomes	becoming	became	become
begin	begins	beginning	began	begun
bend	bends	bending	bent	bent
bet	bets	betting	bet	bet
bite	bites	biting	bit	bitten
bleed	bleeds	bleeding	bled	bled
blow	blows	blowing	blew	blown
break	breaks	breaking	broke	broken
bring	brings	bringing	brought	brought
build	builds	building	built	built
burn	burns	burning	burned	burned
buy	buys	buying	bought	bought
catch	catches	catching	caught	caught
choose	chooses	choosing	chose	chosen
come	comes	coming	came	come
cost	costs	costing	cost	cost
cut	cuts	cutting	cut	cut
deal	deals	dealing	dealt	dealt
dig	digs	digging	dug	dug
draw	draws	drawing	drew	drawn
dream	dreams	dreaming	dreamed	dreamed
drink	drinks	drinking	drank	drunk
drive	drives	driving	drove	driven

eat	eats	eating	ate	eaten
fall	falls	falling	fell	fallen
feed	feeds	feeding	fed	fed
feel	feels	feeling	felt	felt
fight	fights	fighting	fought	fought
find	finds	finding	found	found
fly	flies	flying	flew	flown
forget	forgets	forgetting	forgot	forgotten
forgive	forgives	forgiving	forgave	forgiven
freeze	freezes	freezing	froze	frozen
get	gets	getting	got	got
give	gives	giving	gave	given
go	goes	going	went	gone
grow	grows	growing	grew	grown
hang	hangs	hanging	hung	hung
have	has	having	had	had
hear	hears	hearing	heard	heard
hide	hides	hiding	hid	hidden
hit	hits	hitting	hit	hit
hold	holds	holding	held	held
hurt	hurts	hurting	hurt	hurt
keep	keeps	keeping	kept	kept
know	knows	knowing	knew	known
lay	lays	laying	laid	laid
lead	leads	leading	led	led
learn	learns	learning	learned	learned
leave	leaves	leaving	left	left
lend	lends	lending	lent	lent
let	lets	letting	let	let
lie = body position	lies	lying	lay	lain
lie = say false thing	lies	lying	lied	lied
light	lights	lighting	lit	lit
lose	loses	losing	lost	lost
make	makes	making	made	made
mean	means	meaning	meant	meant
meet	meets	meeting	met	met
pay	pays	paying	paid	paid
put	puts	putting	put	put

quit	quits	quitting	quit	quit
read	reads	reading	read	read
ride	rides	riding	rode	ridden
ring	rings	ringing	rang	rung
run	runs	running	ran	run
say	says	saying	said	said
see	sees	seeing	saw	seen
sell	sells	selling	sold	sold
send	sends	sending	sent	sent
set	sets	setting	set	set
sew	sews	sewing	sewed	sewn
shake	shakes	shaking	shook	shaken
shine	shines	shining	shone	shone
shoot	shoots	shooting	shot	shot
show	shows	showing	showed	shown
shut	shuts	shutting	shut	shut
sing	sings	singing	sang	sung
sit	sits	sitting	sat	sat
sleep	sleeps	sleeping	slept	slept
speak	speaks	speaking	spoke	spoken
spell	spells	spelling	spelled/spelt	spelled/spelt
spend	spends	spending	spent	spent
stand	stands	standing	stood	stood
steal	steals	stealing	stole	stolen
sweep	sweeps	sweeping	swept	swept
swim	swims	swimming	swam	swum
swing	swings	swinging	swung	swung
take	takes	taking	took	taken
teach	teaches	teaching	taught	taught
tear	tears	tearing	tore	torn
tell	tells	telling	told	told
think	thinks	thinking	thought	thought
throw	throws	throwing	threw	thrown
understand	understands	understanding	understood	understood
wake	wakes	waking	woke	woken
wear	wears	wearing	wore	worn
win	wins	winning	won	won
write	writes	writing	wrote	written

Verb tenses

The simple present

The simple present tense is used for things that happen regularly or things that are always true. It is also used to show the speaker's opinions or beliefs.

> They often **go** to the movies on Saturdays.
> He **watches** a lot of TV.
> I **like** coffee for breakfast.
> The sun **rises** in the east.
> They **live** in Canada.
> I **think** he's a very good teacher.

The present continuous

We use the present continuous to talk about things that are happening now, at the time when we are talking.

> I can't go out — I'm **doing** my homework.
> She's **staying** with friends for two weeks.

We also use the present continuous to talk about arrangements for future events.

> I'm **flying** to New York next week.
> I'm **seeing** Milos tonight.

The simple past

The simple past tense is used for single actions in the past.

> I **met** Lucy in the café.
> We **walked** around the park.

It is also used for repeated actions in the past, often with *always*, *never*, or *often*.

> I often **had** lunch with her.
> We always **sent** each other birthday cards.

The present perfect

The present perfect is used to talk about things that happened in the past and continue in the present or at an indefinite time in the past.

> I**'ve known** Julie all my life.
> They **have** already **bought** their tickets.
> **Have** you **bought** your tickets yet?

The past continuous

The past continuous is used to talk about something that was in progress at a certain time in the past. It's used with "while" and the simple past or when two activities were happening at the same time in the past.

> What **were** you **doing** at eight o'clock last night?
> I **was waiting** for a bus, and she **was standing** next to me.
> We **were sitting** in the kitchen when my brother came in.

The future with "going to"

The future with "going to" is used to talk about future plans.

> Tina is **going to** be at the office all day.
> I'm **going to** go shopping this afternoon.

The future with "will"

The future with "will" is used for promises.

> I'**ll** see you tomorrow.
> She'**ll call** you later.

Forming questions

Word order

In statements, the subject usually comes before the first verb, but in questions it comes after the verb.

> His bedroom is big. > Is his bedroom big?
> The weather was good. > Was the weather good?
> The hotel is near here. > Is the hotel near here?

Using "be" to form yes/no questions

Be questions in the present tense use **Is ... ?** and **Are ... ?** For questions about the past, use **Was ... ?** and **Were ... ?**

> **Is** she tall?
> **Are** they very rich?
> **Was** the food good?
> **Were** you pleased?

For questions in the present tense use **Is there ... ?** and **Are there ... ?** For questions about in the past, use **Was there ... ?** and **Were there ... ?**

> **Is there** a mall nearby?
> **Are there** any more chairs?
> **Was there** much noise?
> **Were there** many people there?

Using auxiliary verbs to make yes/no questions

The auxiliary verbs **be**, **have**, and **do** are used to make questions.

We use **do** or **does** to make questions in the simple present, and **did** to make questions in the simple past.

> **Do** you like cheese?
> **Do** they want to come with us?
> **Does** she have enough money?
> **Does** it cost a lot?

> **Did** you see the game?
> **Did** they finish on time?
> **Did** we win?
> **Did** he lock the door?

grammar

We use **am**, **are**, or **is** to make questions in the present continuous, and **was** or **were** to make questions in the past continuous.

> **Am** I doing this right?
> **Are** you working at the moment?
> **Is** he faxing the form?
> **Is** Alicia coming to the meeting?

> **Was** he talking to Jim?
> **Was** the car working?
> **Were** the children playing in the park?
> **Were** they helping?

We use **has** or **have** to make questions in the present perfect.

> **Has** the package arrived yet?
> **Has** Marc finished eating?
> **Have** they given him a new laptop?
> **Have** you seen my keys anywhere?

We use **will** to make questions in the future with "will."

> **Will** you come later?
> **Will** he do the shopping?
> **Will** she go to university?
> **Will** they arrive before ten?

Using modals to make questions

The modal verbs in English are **can**, **could**, **may**, and **would**. Many of them are used to make questions.

> **Can** you speak Polish?
> **Could** they hear me?
> **May** I see the letter?
> **Will** she be able to do it?
> **Would** they come without you?

We do not use **must** in questions. Instead, we say **Do I/we/they have to ... ?**, **Does he/she/it have to ... ?**

> **Do we have to** buy a ticket?
> **Do the dogs have to** stay outside?
> **Does he have to** go to work?
> **Does it have to** be repaired?

Using WH- words to make questions

When you want to get a detailed answer, not just *yes* or *no*, you must use a WH- question. The words **who**, **whose**, **what**, **which**, **when**, **where**, **why**, and **how** are used to form these questions.

> **Who** gave you the money?
> **Whose** shoes are those?
> **What** should I do with these books?
> **Which** plates should I use?
> **When** did you leave college?
> **Where** is Lucy?
> **Why** do they look so unhappy?
> **How** can I earn more money?

Using your voice to make questions

When you are speaking, you can often use the tone of your voice to make what you are saying into a question, especially if your question shows surprise, or if you want to make sure about something. To do this, the tone must rise at the end of the sentence.

> She's still not here?
> It's your birthday?
> You're sure you don't want more to eat?
> I can take all these?

Short forms

We often use short forms of words in conversation, for example **I'm** (I am), **he'll** (he will), **didn't** (did not). These forms are also used in informal writing.

We use an apostrophe (') to represent the missing letters.

These are the short forms we use.

> 'm = am
> 's = is *or* has
> 're = are
> 've = have
> 'll = will
> 'd = would *or* had

> **I'm** very happy.
> **They're** having a party.
> **We've** finished our work.
> **He'll** call you later.

's can mean either **is** or **has**.

> **John's** busy at the moment. (= John is)
> **Here's** your coat. (= here is)
> **She's** seen it before. (= she has)
> **Who's** finished their work? (= who has)

'd can mean either **would** or **had**.

> **I'd** like a cup of tea. (= I would)
> He said **he'd** do it later. (= he would)
> **She'd** already gone shopping by the time I got there. (= she had)
> **They'd** lost their phone before they got on the bus. (= they had)

Short forms in negatives

Short forms are also used for negatives made with the auxiliary verbs (**be**, **have**, and **do**), and with modals such as **can**, **will**, and **must**.

be	have	do
isn't = is not	**haven't** = have not	**don't** = do not
aren't = are not	**hasn't** = has not	**doesn't** = does not
wasn't = was not	**hadn't** = had not	**didn't** = did not
weren't = were not		

> My house **isn't** far from here.
> We **weren't** doing anything wrong.
> I **haven't** been to the U.S.
> She **hasn't** seen the movie.
> I **don't** know anything about it.
> They **didn't** like the food.

These are the common negative short forms made with modals.

can't = cannot **couldn't** = could not	**shouldn't** = should not

> You **can't** go inside the building.
> We **couldn't** find him.
> I **shouldn't** eat so much.

Count and noncount nouns

Count nouns are the words for things that we can count. They have singular and plural forms. They can have **a** or **an** in front of them. If they are singular, they *must* have a word like **a**, **an**, **the**, or **his** in front of them.

> She ate **an apple**.
> I sat on **the chair**.
> Where should I put **my coat**?
> Would you like **a cookie**?

Noncount nouns are the words for things that cannot be counted. They cannot have **a** or **an** in front of them, and they do not have a plural form.

> I didn't have enough money to buy two tickets.
> I asked for her **advice**.
> Mix the **water** with the **flour**.
> We were enjoying the **sunshine**.

Here are some very common noncount nouns.

advice	furniture	meat
air	happiness	money
anger	homework	music
beauty	information	safety
behavior	knowledge	water
damage	luggage	work

Be careful with noncount nouns. Remember that the verb that goes with them must be singular.

> The **meat was** not cooked properly.
> The **damage has** not been repaired.
> The **information** he gave us **was** correct.
> Her **behavior upsets** everyone.

Some/any

You can use **some** and **any** with plural count nouns and with noncount nouns.

> I'd like **some potatoes**.
> I don't have **any pencils** with me.
> We need to buy **some furniture**.
> Do you have **any milk**?

Many/a few

You can use **many** and **a few** with plural count nouns, but not with noncount nouns.

> There aren't **many stores** in the village.
> I've never seen so **many planes!**
> There were only **a few sandwiches** left.
> We waited for **a few minutes**.

Much

You can use **much** with noncount nouns, but not with count nouns.

> You've given me too **much rice**.
> I don't have **much experience** of working in an office.

A lot of

You can use **a lot of** with plural count nouns and with noncount nouns.

> I ate **a lot of cookies**.
> He has visited **a lot of countries**.
> She spent **a lot of money**.
> There was **a lot of laughter**.

Phrasal verbs

Phrasal verbs

Phrasal verbs such as **get up** and **come in** are very common in English. They are formed with a main verb and a particle (a preposition or an adverb). Here are some very common phrasal verbs which are useful to learn.

break down to stop working
> *The car broke down.*
> *Our washing machine broke down.*

call (someone) back to call someone in return for a call they made to you
> *I'll call you back.*
> *Could you call back later?*

calm down to become less upset or excited
> *Calm down and listen to me.*
> *We'd better give him time to calm down.*

cheer (someone) up to start feeling happier or to make someone feel happier
> *I brought flowers to cheer her up.*
> *We cheered up as soon as we saw our hotel.*

come in to enter a place
> *Come in and sit down.*
> *Everyone stood up when the teacher came in.*

do something over to do again
> *He did it over and over until he got it right.*
> *I had to do my report over because I accidentally deleted it the first time.*

fall down if a person falls over, they fall to the ground, and if an object falls over, it falls onto its side
> *I tripped on a branch and fell down.*
> *I knocked the vase and it fell down.*

fill something out to write information in the spaces on a form
> *When you have filled out the form, send it to your employer.*
> *I had to fill out an application for a visa.*

find out to learn the facts about something
> I'll watch the next episode and find out what happens.
> She broke the window and worried that her mother would find out.

get over something to become happy and well again after an unhappy experience or an illness
> It took me a long time to get over losing my MP3 player.
> I can't go running until I get over this cold.

get up to get out of bed
> They have to get up early in the morning.
> I hate getting up!

give in to agree to do something although you do not really want to do it
> After saying "no" a hundred times, I finally gave in and said "yes."
> We will not give in to their demands.

give up to decide that you cannot do something and stop trying to do it
> I give up – I'll never understand this.
> It was hard for Penny to climb the mountain, but she never thought of giving up.

give up something to stop doing or having something
> I have decided to give up eating meat.
> I had to give up running because of my knees.

grow up to gradually change from being a child into being an adult.
> She grew up in Shanghai.
> When he grows up, he wants to be a doctor.

hurry up to do something more quickly
> Hurry up and get ready, or you'll miss the school bus.
> I need to hurry up and get this work finished.

join in (something) to start to take part in an activity with other people
> I started singing, and everyone else joined in.
> He never joined in our discussions.

keep on doing something to continue to do something or to do something many times

>*I asked them to be quiet, but they kept on talking.*
>*She kept on asking silly questions.*

leave someone/something out to not include someone or something

>*Why did they leave her out of the discussion?*
>*I made the cake, but I left out the nuts because I don't like them.*

look after someone/something to take care of someone or something

>*Maria looks after the children while I'm at work.*
>*Could you look after my plants when I'm on vacation?*

look forward to something to want something to happen because you think you will enjoy it

>*She's looking forward to her vacation in Hawaii.*
>*I was looking forward to relaxing.*

make something up to invent something

>*It was all lies. I made it all up.*
>*We made up a new game.*

pick someone/something up to collect someone or something from a place, often in a car

>*Please could you pick me up at 5:00?*
>*She went home to pick up some clean clothes.*

put something away to put something back in the place where it is usually kept

>*Kyle put the milk away in the refrigerator.*
>*I put away all the clean clothes.*

put something on to place clothing on your body in order to wear it

>*Stacey put her coat on and went out.*
>*I decided to put on my boots.*

run out (of something) to have no more of something left

>*We ran out of milk this morning.*
>*I need to get bread before we run out.*

sit down to move your body down until you are sitting on something

> *Please sit down and make yourself comfortable.*
> *I sat down on the rock.*

take back/return

> *He returned the laptop because it didn't have a battery.*
> *The jacket was too small, so Elise took it back.*

take off used for saying that an airplane leaves the ground and starts flying

> *We took off at 11 o'clock.*
> *When did the plane take off?*

take off/to remove something

> *It was very hot inside, so Fred took off his sweater.*
> *They asked me to take off my shoes.*

wake up to stop sleeping

> *I woke up early.*
> *What time do you normally wake up?*